Abschlussprüfung
Englisch

von Petra Schappert
unter Mitarbeit der Verlagsredaktion

Fachoberschule
Hessen

Cornelsen

Abschlussprüfung Englisch
Fachoberschule Hessen

Verfasserin
Petra Schappert, Stuttgart

Kritische Durchsicht
Liane Krug, Homberg

Redaktion
Kari-ann Warnakulasuriya

Außenredaktion
Neil Porter

Umschlaggestaltung
hawemannundmosch, konzeption und gestaltung, Berlin

Layout
Ingo Ostermaier

Technische Umsetzung
Stephan Hilleckenbach, Berlin

www.cornelsen.de

Die Webseiten Dritter, deren Internetadressen in diesem Lehrwerk angegeben sind, wurden vor Drucklegung sorgfältig geprüft. Der Verlag übernimmt keine Gewähr für die Aktualität und den Inhalt dieser Seiten oder solcher, die mit ihnen verlinkt sind.

1. Auflage, 1. Druck 2017

Alle Drucke dieser Auflage sind inhaltlich unverändert und können im Unterricht nebeneinander verwendet werden.

© 2017 Cornelsen Verlag GmbH, Berlin

Druck: Heenemann, Berlin

ISBN 978-3-06-451525-3

PEFC zertifiziert
Dieses Produkt stammt aus nachhaltig bewirtschafteten Wäldern und kontrollierten Quellen.
www.pefc.de
PEFC/04-31-1158

INHALT

Einleitung

FÜR WEN DIESES ARBEITSBUCH IST

Dieses Arbeitsbuch ist für Schülerinnen und Schüler bestimmt, die an der zentralen Abschlussprüfung der Fachoberschule im Fach Englisch in Hessen teilnehmen wollen. Die Aufgaben in diesem Heft bereiten systematisch auf alle Teile der schriftlichen Prüfung vor.

DIE STRUKTUR DES ARBEITSBUCHES

Musterprüfungen: Der erste Teil enthält vier Musterprüfungen. Diese Musterprüfungen sind so aufgebaut wie die Musterprüfungen des Hessischen Kultusministeriums und die Prüfung im ersten Durchlauf.

Training: Der zweite Teil, der Trainingsteil, enthält ausführliche Erläuterungen zu allen Aufgabentypen der Prüfung, Beispielaufgaben zu allen wesentlichen Varianten der Prüfung gemäß des Prüfungserlasses sowie Schritte zur Herangehensweise, Tipps zur effektiven Bearbeitung und Hinweise auf häufige Fehler.

Mit diesen Übungen kann keine authentische Prüfungssituation geschaffen werden, aber sie werden Ihnen helfen, sich an den Ablauf und die Formulierungen der Prüfung zu gewöhnen und effektiv bei der Bearbeitung der Aufgaben vorzugehen. Bearbeiten Sie diese Übungen in Ihrem eigenen Arbeitsrhythmus und – falls gewünscht – mithilfe Ihrer Lehrbücher und Wörterbücher.

Sie können den Trainingsteil entweder systematisch von Anfang bis Ende durcharbeiten, oder Sie suchen sich die Bereiche aus, die Sie besonders üben möchten. Die Musterprüfungen können Sie vorab durcharbeiten, sozusagen als Diagnose Ihres Lernstandes, oder im Anschluss an den Trainingsteil, um Ihren Lernfortschritt zu testen. Sie können auch zwischendurch immer mal wieder eine Musterprüfung bearbeiten, um zu sehen, wo noch Schwierigkeiten bestehen. Sinnvoll ist sicherlich auch, an den Aufgabentypen zu arbeiten, die Ihnen Ihrer Einschätzung nach am meisten Probleme bereiten.

Themenwortschatz: Hier werden Listen von für die Prüfung relevanten Wörter angeboten.

Operatoren: Hier finden Sie alle Operatoren, die in die Aufgaben verwendet werden.

Lösungsheft: Das beiliegende Lösungsheft enthält Lösungen bzw. Lösungsvorschläge für die Musterprüfungen und alle Übungen im Trainingsteil sowie die Transkripte der Hörtexte. Schlagen Sie die Lösungen erst nach, wenn Sie die Aufgabe selbst bearbeitet haben oder falls Sie nicht weiterkommen. Alles andere verleitet dazu, ständig nachzuschlagen oder gleich die Lösungen abzuschreiben. Dadurch wird der Lerneffekt deutlich reduziert.

 Dieses Symbol weist auf Audios zum Download: Einfach auf www.cornelsen.de/webcodes gehen, den Webcode FOSHESSEN-Audio aufrufen und auf den Link zu den Audiodateien klicken.

Auf der gegenüberliegenden Seite erhalten Sie alle Informationen zur Prüfung auf einen Blick.

Und nun viel Spaß bei der Prüfungsvorbereitung – und natürlich viel Erfolg bei der Prüfung!

Die Prüfung auf einen Blick

Sie erhalten zwei Vorschläge zur Auswahl.
Auswahlzeit: 30 Minuten
Bearbeitungszeit: 180 Minuten

In der Prüfung steht Ihnen Folgendes zur Verfügung:
– ein Wörterbuch der deutschen Rechtschreibung
– ein zweisprachiges Klausurwörterbuch mit zwischen 120.000 und 180.000 Stichwörtern und Redewendungen
– ein einsprachiges englisches Wörterbuch
– eine Liste der Operatoren

Fertigkeit	Formales	Aufgabentyp	Punkte
Hörverstehen	Der Hörtext bzw. die Hörtexte dauern insgesamt 3 bis 6 Minuten. Sie werden zweimal vorgespielt, mit einer Pause von 2 Minuten.	Kann aus folgenden Aufgabentypen bestehen: ■ Multiple Choice ■ Ausfüllen eines Formulars ■ Ausfüllen einer Tabelle/Übersicht mit kurzen Informationen oder Stichpunkten ■ Zuordnungsaufgabe ■ Wiedergabe der Hauptpunkte des Hörtextes auf Deutsch oder Englisch ■ Beantwortung von Fragen auf Deutsch oder Englisch ■ Vervollständigen von Teilsätzen	15 BE
Leseverstehen	Die schriftliche Textvorlage umfasst ca. 300 bis 500 Wörter.	Kann aus folgenden Aufgabentypen bestehen: ■ Multiple Choice ■ Ausfüllen eines Formulars ■ Ausfüllen einer Tabelle/Übersicht mit kurzen Informationen oder Stichpunkten ■ Zuordnungsaufgabe ■ Wiedergabe der Hauptpunkte der Textvorlage auf Deutsch oder Englisch ■ Beantwortung von Fragen auf Deutsch oder Englisch ■ Vervollständigen von Teilsätzen	15 BE
Mediation		Besteht aus den beiden folgenden Aufgabentypen: ■ sinngemäße Übersetzung von Englisch nach Deutsch ■ Zusammenfassung eines deutschen Textes in englischer Sprache	15 BE 15 BE
Produktion	Sie verfassen einen Text mit einer Länge von 270 bis 330 Wörtern.	Besteht aus einem der folgenden Aufgabentypen: ■ Kommentar ■ Diskussion/Vergleich ■ Beschreibung und Interpretation eines Bildes/Cartoons/Diagramms	40 BE

MUSTERPRÜFUNGEN

MUSTERPRÜFUNG 1

 ### 1 Hörverstehen

Im ersten Teil der Prüfung wird Ihr Hörverständnis geprüft. Der Hörtext beträgt zwischen 3 und 6 Minuten. Hier können unterschiedliche Aufgaben gestellt werden: die Wiedergabe der Hauptpunkte des Hörtextes auf Deutsch oder Englisch, das Beantworten von Fragen auf Deutsch oder Englisch, das Vervollständigen von Teilsätzen, Multiple-Choice-Aufgaben, das Ausfüllen eines Formulars oder das Ausfüllen einer Tabelle mit kurzen Informationen bzw. Stichpunkten.

Tipps zur Vorgehensweise

1. Schritt: Lesen Sie sich die Aufgaben aufmerksam durch. Unterstreichen Sie zentrale Wörter. So wissen Sie, worauf Sie beim Hören achten müssen.

2. Schritt: Versuchen Sie nicht, beim Hören jedes einzelne Wort zu verstehen. Das Gesamtverständnis ist wichtiger. Wenn Sie einem unbekannten Wort gedanklich nachhängen, bekommen Sie den Rest des Hörtextes nicht mehr mit.

3. Schritt: Wenn Sie sich Notizen machen, müssen Sie nicht auf eine korrekte Rechtschreibung oder Grammatik achten. Kritzeln Sie einfach mit. Wenn Sie die Notizen später übertragen, können Sie immer noch auf sprachliche Korrektheit achten.

4. Schritt: Überprüfen Sie beim zweiten Hören, ob Sie alles richtig gemacht haben.

Listen to the audio file and complete the table with the relevant information in English based on the information you hear. **(15 BE)**

event on November 28th (2 BE)	
participants (1 BE)	
necessity of the event (4 BE)	
achievements during the event (2 BE)	

current important topics (2 BE)	
reasons for the topics being important (2 BE)	
consequences of the event (2 BE)	

2 Leseverstehen

Im zweiten Teil der Prüfung wird Ihr Leseverstehen geprüft. Der Text besteht aus 300–500 Wörtern. Hier müssen unterschiedliche Aufgaben erledigt werden: die Wiedergabe der Hauptpunkte des Textes auf Deutsch oder Englisch, das Beantworten von Fragen auf Deutsch oder Englisch, das Vervollständigen von Teilsätzen, Multiple-Choice-Aufgaben, das Ausfüllen eines Formulars oder einer Tabelle mit kurzen Informationen bzw. Stichpunkten oder das Zuordnen von Aussagen aus dem Text zuordnen (*matching*).

Tipps zur Vorgehensweise

1. Schritt: Lesen Sie den Text zuerst einmal zügig durch. Lassen Sie sich von schwierigen Passagen nicht entmutigen. Wenn Sie etwas beim ersten Lesen nicht verstehen, lesen Sie trotzdem weiter. Wenn Sie den gesamten Text gelesen haben, ergibt sich manches aus dem Zusammenhang.

2. Schritt: Lesen Sie nun die Aufgabenstellung aufmerksam durch und nehmen Sie sich dann den Text ein zweites Mal vor. Diesmal sollten Sie gründlicher lesen. Markieren Sie im Text die Passagen, die erkennbar durch Wortwahl/Zahlen/Namen/Fakten usw. für die Aufgabe von Bedeutung sind.

3. Schritt: Überprüfen Sie nun noch einmal genau, ob die jeweiligen Passagen wirklich zur richtigen Lösung führen. Achten Sie bei Multiple-Choice-Aufgaben besonders auf die einzelnen Wörter, denn welche Aussage die richtige ist, hängt oft von Kleinigkeiten ab.

Read the text (Material 1, p. 10) and complete the table below with the relevant information in German. **(15 BE)**

Wofür stehen Luftballons normalerweise? (1 BE)	
Was haben Kinder in Bangladesch mit Lufballons zu tun? (3 BE)	
Wann beginnt und endet ihr Arbeitstag? (2 BE)	
Warum arbeiten so viele Kinder für so wenig Geld? (3 BE)	
Wie viele Kinder arbeiten in Bangladesch? (2 BE)	
Wo arbeiten die Kinder? (1 BE)	
Unter welchen Arbeitsbedingungen arbeiten viele Kinder? (2 BE)	
Welche Konsequenzen hat die Arbeit für die Kinder? (1 BE)	

3 Mediation

3.1 Translate the text excerpt (Material 2, p. 10) including the title freely into German. Remember to translate as closely as possible and as freely as necessary. **(15 BE)**

Tipps zur Vorgehensweise

1. Schritt: Lesen Sie den Text sorgfältig durch und schlagen Sie die Ihnen unbekannten Wörter nach. Markieren Sie knifflige Satz- oder Grammatikkonstruktionen und schwierige Wörter, auf die Sie beim Übersetzen besonders achten müssen.

2. Schritt: Übersetzen Sie nun den Text Satz für Satz ins Deutsche. Übersetzen Sie so genau wie möglich, aber so frei wie nötig. Die Übersetzung muss sich wie ein in Deutsch verfasster Text lesen.

3.2 Summarize the text (Material 3, p. 11) in English in not more than 120 words. One point (1 BE) will be deducted for every 10 words that you are over the word limit. Please count your words in groups of 10. **(15 BE)**

Tipps zur Vorgehensweise

1. Schritt: Lesen Sie den Text sorgfältig durch und kennzeichnen Sie die in Frage kommenden Informationen, indem Sie Passagen markieren oder unterstreichen. Sie können auch Notizen an den Rand schreiben. Strukturieren Sie Ihre Notizen, z. B. als Mind Map, und ordnen Sie dann Ihre Ergebnisse den vorher unterstrichenen Schlüsselbegriffen in der Aufgabenstellung zu.

2. Schritt: Übertragen Sie nun die von Ihnen gefundenen Informationen aus dem Text ins Englische. Übersetzen Sie dabei nicht Wort für Wort.

4 Produktion

Tipps zur Vorgehensweise

1. Schritt: Lesen Sie sich die Aufgabe gründlich durch und markieren Sie die Schlüsselwörter bezogen auf Inhalt und Operatoren.

2. Schritt: Bevor Sie mit dem Schreiben beginnen, nehmen Sie sich Zeit für die Planung. Überlegen Sie sich, wie Sie Ihren Text aufbauen: Womit wollen Sie beginnen? Ein guter Einstieg ist besonders wichtig. Was wäre eine gute Gliederung Ihres Textes? Wenn Sie eine Stellungnahme schreiben, entscheiden Sie zunächst: Mit welchen Argumenten beginnen Sie? Welche Argumente bauen gut aufeinander auf? Auch bei einer Bildbeschreibung sollten Sie auf eine gute Struktur achten. Beginnen Sie mit einer Einleitung, beschreiben Sie dann, was Sie auf dem Bild sehen, und interpretieren Sie das Bild, bevor Sie abschließend Stellung nehmen.

Auch hier gilt, wie bei allen anderen Aufgaben:

Am Schluss sollten Sie Ihren Text noch einmal durchlesen und auf korrekte Grammatik und Rechtschreibung überprüfen!

Comment on sustainable shopping as described in the article "Es geht noch billiger als mit Billigklamotten" (Material 3, p. 11) considering what consumption in the western world has to do with poverty in third-world countries.

Write 270–330 words.
Two points (2 BE) will be deducted for every 15 words that you are below or over the word limit.
Please count your words in groups of 50. **(40 BE)**

Material 1

Bangladeshi children forced to work in factories making party balloons

For children around the world, brightly-coloured balloons signify celebration. Unless, that is, they are among the Bangladeshi children covered in dust who spend their lives working in the balloon factories. The children, some as young as 10, should be at school. Instead, they are in the dirty factory, sorting the balloons into colours and carrying loads too heavy for their young arms.

Their day starts at 6am, and continues for 11 hours, finally being released at 5pm.

And for their trouble and hard work, they are rewarded with as little as £6.50 a month. At best, they can expect £16.

That is significantly less than the £41.80 minimum wage for entry level garment workers set by the government in the wake of the Rana Plaza disaster, in which more than 1,100 people died.

But many Bangladeshi families have little choice but to send their children out to work. The practice is so common the money is handed straight to the child's family.

Twelve-year-old Apu, a labourer in a balloon factories, is one such child.

"My father left me and my mum when I was five," he explained. "My mother takes care of me since then. Now I am working to help my mother."

Fellow balloon factory worker Ruma, 11, told a similar story of woe – although he was glad to no longer be in school. "I don't like to study," he said. "My father is a daily wage labourer but his earnings are not enough for us. I am helping them financially by working in here."

Across Bangladesh, it is thought there are about a million children aged 10 to 14 working as child labourers, according to UNICEF [...].

"In Bangladesh there are nearly five million children between the age of 5 and 14 working in hazardous conditions in factories, garages and homes, in railway stations and markets [...] – many for little or no pay at all," said photographer Zakir Chowdhury. "Many boys and girls who work do not have access to education and become trapped in low-skilled, low-pay work that further binds them into the cycle of poverty."

Others, however, appear not to think of it as a problem, including balloon factory owner Zakir Hossain, who set his business up with the help of his wife and eldest son. He freely admits to employing children to work for him, but says they are treated well.

Mr Hossain said: "In my factory all children labour like my son does, I give the same opportunity to all of them. They work here to help their families' lives, but in my mind I think they are children of other parents like me. I wish they will be educated in future and become self-dependent." Wife Beauty added: "If we didn't give the opportunity for children to work here, they would be thieving or snatching – here it is better and the children's families feel safe."

(Source: Flora Drury, The Daily Mail, 8 September 2015; 493 words)

Material 2

Why you need to use your "environmentally friendly" cotton carrier bag 131 times to be green

Cotton bags offered by many supermarkets may be less "green" than plastic carriers – and may cause more global warming, according to scientists. As a greater amount of energy goes

5 into making a cloth carrier than a polythene one, a cotton bag has to be used 131 times before it has the same environmental impact than its plastic counterpart. But most of us only use the bags around 51 times before they 10 are thrown away, researchers found.

Paper bags need to be used three times to fall below the environmental impact of the thin plastic carrier, while bags for life – made of stronger plastic – have to be used four times to 15 start having less ecological impact.

Using a thin plastic bag – made from a plastic called high-density polyethylene (HDPE) – equates to generating 1.57kg of carbon dioxide, the greenhouse gas that scientist believe leads 20 to global warming according to the report. A cotton bag would have to be re-used 171 times

to emit the same level of CO_2. Cotton bags typically made in China have a greater environmental impact because of the water and fertiliser required in their production, as 25 well as their transportation and greater weight.

The Daily Mail, through its "Banish the Bags" campaign has spearheaded efforts to avoid using plastic bags wherever possible to save 30 the environment.

Peter Woodall, speaking on behalf of the Packaging and Films Association, which represents plastic bag makers, said: "It comes down to reducing, reusing and recycling." 35

(Source: Colin Fernandez, The Daily Mail, 21 February 2011; 264 words)

Material 3

Es geht noch billiger als mit Billigklamotten

Wie wäre das: jede Woche ein neues Kleidungsstück im Schrank - modisch, umweltfreundlich, für null Euro. Eine wirre Ökofantasie? Nein, das ist längst möglich. Zum Beispiel 5 so: An einem warmen Samstag strömten im Juni rund 10.000 Menschen zu sogenannten Kleidertauschpartys in ganz Deutschland. Das Konzept: mit zehn aussortierten Kleidungsstücken hingehen, mit zehn gebrauchten Klei- 10 dungsstücken heimgehen. Laut einer Greenpeace-Erhebung werden von den 5,2 Milliarden Kleidungsstücken in unseren Kleiderschränken 40 Prozent sehr selten oder nie getragen, jeder Achte trägt seine Schuhe nicht einmal 15 zwölf Monate lang. Zugleich geben die Deutschen immer mehr Geld für Textilien aus, obwohl es die zu immer niedrigeren Preisen gibt. Kurzum: Wir verbrauchen Kleidung wie Pappbecher.

20 Eine Armada von Aktivisten, Behörden und Non-Profit-Organisationen hält dagegen: Sie werben für Nachhaltigkeit, decken Textilskandale auf, prüfen Sozialstandards und verleihen Umweltsiegel. Doch ist nachhaltige Mode

nicht viel spießiger, hässlicher und zudem 25 auch noch teurer als die neueste Kollektion im Textildiscounter? Über Geschmack lässt sich natürlich streiten, aber es gibt etliche Alternativen zum piefigen Gebrauchtwarenmarkt im Gemeindezentrum. Einige Designer haben 30 sich etwa aufs sogenannte Upcycling spezialisiert, also darauf, aus Abfallmaterialien trendige Mode zu kreieren. So gibt es Labels, die Shirts aus Brennnesseln und Pullover aus Plastikflaschen herstellen – andere verzichten 35 komplett auf Baumwolle, Billiglöhne oder Chemikalien.

Der Markt für alternative Mode-Unternehmen ist klein, wächst aber seit einigen Jahren. Klamotten lassen sich inzwischen problemlos 40 tauschen (beispielsweise über den „Kleiderkreisel"), ausleihen (etwa in der „Kleiderei") oder selbst herstellen (sogar aus Müll). Ach ja, und dann gibt es natürlich noch die Kleidertauschpartys – in Hamburg zum Beispiel schon 45 wieder am 5. Dezember.

(Source: Peter Maxwill, Der Spiegel, 3 December 2015; 263 words)

MUSTERPRÜFUNG 2

1 Hörverstehen

Listen to the audio file and complete the table with the relevant information in English based on the information you hear.

(15 BE)

recent development concerning prices (1 BE)	
main things affecting the price of food (4 BE)	
importance of oil for food prices (3 BE)	
uses for corn (3 BE)	
consequences of improved living standards in India and China (2 BE)	
two factors that would lead to cheaper food prices (2 BE)	

2 Leseverstehen

Read the text (Material 1, p. 15) and work on the tasks below in English.   **(15 BE)**

2.1 The gadgets that are illegally transported to Africa are ... (*Name four.*)

_____

_____ (2 BE)

2.2 Complete the sentences below.

This happens because _____

_____ (2 BE)

In Africa the electronic gadgets are _____

_____ (3 BE)

2.3 Other components of this electronic scrap are ... (*Name four.*)

_____

_____ (2 BE)

2.4 Complete the sentences below.

People come into contact with these substances because _____

_____ (2 BE)

Britain ranks position number five concerning ...[a] and position number six concerning ...[b]

a _____

b _____ (2 BE)

2.6 Tick the correct answer according to the text.

The solution to e-waste is ... (1 BE)

☐ to buy more sustainable products.

☐ to produce less waste.

☐ to minimize consumption and increase recycling.

☐ to increase prices for electric gadgets.

The wealthiest nations of Europe ... (1 BE)

☐ are the biggest exporters of e-waste.

☐ produce the largest amount of e-waste per head of population.

☐ are part of the European Union.

☐ do the most to recycle their waste.

3 Mediation

3.1 Translate the text (Material 2, p. 16) including the title freely into German.
Remember to translate as closely as possible and as freely as necessary.   **(15 BE)**

3.2 Summarize the text (Material 3, p. 16) in English in not more than 120 words.
One point (1 BE) will be deducted for every 10 words that you are over the word limit.
Please count your words in groups of 10.   **(15 BE)**

4 Produktion

Describe the cartoon and interpret the message of the cartoon (Material 4, p. 17) concerning globalization and the environment.

Write 270–330 words.

Two points (2 BE) will be deducted for every 15 words that you are over the word limit.
Please count your words in groups of 50.   **(40 BE)**

Material 1

Where your computer goes to die

Thousands of broken televisions, computers, microwaves and refrigerators are being illegally exported to African countries and dumped in gigantic landfills like Agbogbloshie
5 in Ghana because it costs less than recycling them in their countries of origin. [...]

When massive containers arrive in Ghana and Nigeria, they are trucked to remote locations where the locals can buy the products directly
10 without testing them to later sell in markets, Dr Ruediger Kuehr told MailOnline. "The reasoning behind it is quite simple – economic and financial. Recycling in the European Union and the UK costs money. So if a broker successfully
15 collects enough material and sends it to Africa, it could be in their interest because people in Africa are still paying for this."

The waste discarded in 2014 contained around 300 tonnes of gold, 16 million tonnes of iron
20 and nearly two million tonnes of copper as well as significant amounts of silver, aluminium and palladium.

And alarmingly, it also contained "substantial amounts" of life-threatening toxic material
25 like mercury and cadmium which can cause organ failure and severe mental impairment if they pollute the local water supply.

In the deadly fields of Agbogbloshie, photographer Yepoka Yeebo has seen young
30 men braving toxic fumes and explosive appliances in what she deems "the chaotic heart of one of west Africa's biggest economies".

She has witnessed boys as young as 14 trawling
35 barefoot through acres of what could be deadly waste material which may cause them irreparable harm.

Yepoka adds: "The electronic waste leaks lead, mercury, arsenic, zinc and flame-retardants. They've been found in toxic concentrations in 40 the air, water, and even on the fruits and vegetables at the wholesale market." [...]

The UK was identified as one of the world's largest generators of e-waste and ranked fifth in the world in terms of material discarded per 45 person, with each Briton producing 23.5kg every year.

It also produced the sixth most e-waste overall and its 1.5 megatons of waste was only 100,000 tonnes less than India which has 20 times the 50 population.

A United Nations University (UNU) report said that only one-third of e-waste in the UK is recycled through recognised schemes, a figure that must reach 85 per cent by 2019 under 55 European Union rules. According to the Independent, UNU researcher Federico Magalini said: "In the UK we are seeing that the 'lifespan' of an electric or electronic product may be particularly short. We should not 60 simply try to stop consumption to minimise the amount of waste being generated, but should instead make sure that it is properly collected and recycled."

The weight of last year's e-waste is comparable 65 to over 1.1 million 18-wheel trucks – enough to form a line from New York to Tokyo and back.

While the US and China produce almost a third of the world's combined e-waste, the top producers per-capita are the wealthy nations 70 of northern and western Europe – the top five being Norway, Switzerland, Iceland, Denmark, and the UK.

(Source: Jay Akbar, The Daily Mail, 23 April 2015; 500 words)

Material 2

Love across the divide: interracial relationships growing in Britain

The UK is becoming a racial melting pot with a surge in the number of relationships and marriages across ethnic dividing lines in the last decade, according to official figures.

5 But while the number of people from black, Asian and mixed-race backgrounds settling down with someone from another group have all risen, white people remain by far the most segregated on the domestic front. New analysis 10 of census figures shows that the number of people in England and Wales living with or married to someone from another group jumped 35 per cent to 2.3 million in the 10-years up to the last census. During that period the 15 number of people described on census forms as "mixed" or "multiple" ethnicity almost doubled from just 660,000 in 2001 to 1.2 million in 2011, making it by far the fastest growing category.

Overall almost one in 10 people living in Britain 20 is married to or living with someone from outside their own ethnic group, the analysis from the Office for National Statistics shows. [...]

The contrast between white people and other 25 communities echoes the findings of the Social Integration Commission, a study published earlier this week, which showed that white people are the least integrated with other groups in their social lives. 30

The study, which analysed the friendship groups of 4,000 people, noted that a typical white person mixes with 50 per cent fewer people from other groups as might be expected given the make-up of where they live. 35

(Source: John Bingham, The Daily Telegraph, 3 July 2014; 255 words)

Material 3

Aufleben der stillen Minen?

Harlan County im bergigen Osten des US-Bundesstaates Kentucky ist das Herz der Appalachen. In den Bergen lagert viel Kohle. [...] Im beschaulichen Dorf Lynch wohnten einmal 5 rund 10.000 Menschen, es gab Schulen, ein Krankenhaus, Geschäfte – alles weg. Vielleicht 200 Einwohner haben ausgeharrt. Einer von ihnen ist John. „Die Kohleindustrie ist am Boden. Deshalb wurde ich auch entlassen. Im 10 Harlan County bist du entweder zum Militär gegangen, bist Bergmann geworden oder bist zur Schule gegangen", sagt John.

Keine Frage: Obamas „Clean Power Plan" ist schuld am Niedergang der Kohle, wenigstens 15 mitverantwortlich. Neben der modernen Technologie, neben dem billigen Erdgas, das dank Fracking in Texas und North Dakota in Hülle und Fülle vorhanden ist. Der jetzige US-Präsident Donald Trump könnte helfen – mit freier 20 Fahrt für die Kohle.

In Lynch ist das durchschnittliche Jahreseinkommen auf weniger als 20.000 Dollar pro Jahr gesunken. Deshalb will Sandy an eine Renaissance der Kohle glauben, deshalb gefällt ihr Trumps Politik. 25

Damit folgt Hodges wie fast alle Menschen im Osten Kentuckys der Logik von Trump. Ausbeutung fossiler Brennstoffe und der Schutz der Umwelt stellen für sie keinen Gegensatz dar. 30

Dee Davis sieht das anders. Er leitet das Büro für ländliche Entwicklung in Whitesburg, Kentucky. „Keine Frage, die Dinge sind hier rau. Der Kohleboom ist ziemlich am Ende. Überhaupt gibt es auf der Welt nicht besonders viele pros- 35 perierende Kohlegemeinden. Kohle macht die Bergleute nicht reich", sagt Davis. Wenn das „Kohlekapital" zu Ende gehe, müsse man überlegen, was kommt. „Man könnte sagen: Die Kohle war unser Freund, sie ist aber definitiv 40 nicht unsere Zukunft", fasst der Büroleiter zusammen.

Trotzdem: Trumps Kohlepolitik wird von der Mehrheit der Menschen im Osten Kentuckys
45 begrüßt, denn immer wieder versprachen Präsidenten in den vergangenen 60 Jahren, etwas

für die verarmende Region zu tun, einen Ersatz für die wegfallenden Kohlejobs zu schaffen. Den gibt es bis heute nicht.

(Source: Andreas Horchler, www.tagesschau.de, 29 March 2017; 308 words)

Material 4

WE ALL HAVE TO MAKE SACRIFICES FOR THE ENVIRONMENT..**AND YOU'RE OURS!**

(Source: cartoonstock/Fran)

Musterprüfung 3

1 Hörverstehen

Listen to the audio file and complete the table with the relevant information in English based on the information you hear.

(15 BE)

description of experiment (1 BE)	
intended goal (2 BE)	
success/development of the experiment (3 BE)	
contents of the basement (4 BE)	
contents of the paper box (1 BE)	
plans for the paper (2 BE)	
friends' suggestion what to do with some of the garbage (1 BE)	
garbage as a symbol (1 BE)	

2 Leseverstehen

Please read the text (Material 1, p. 21) and work on the tasks below in English. **(15 BE)**

2.1 Complete the sentences below.

Omar's current occupation is … _____

_____ (1 BE)

The journalist Kermani talked to Omar … _____ (1 BE)

Omar told Kermani … _____

_____ (2 BE)

Kermani's impression of Omar was that of a … _____

_____ (2 BE)

Omar considers his childhood to have been … _____ (1 BE)

Rashad Ali says that young men who tend to radicalism … _____

_____ (2 BE)

Omar thinks his task in Syria is to … _____

_____ (3 BE)

Ismael Lea South says the IS is "attractive" because … _____

_____ (2 BE)

2.2 Tick the correct answer according to the text.

Young Muslims in Great Britain … (1 BE)

☐ feel well-integrated.

☐ don't like non-Muslims.

☐ feel that there is a gap between them and non-Muslims.

☐ think that Muslims and non-Muslims get along well.

3 Mediation

3.1 Translate the text excerpt (Material 2, p. 22) including the headline freely into German. Remember to translate as closely as possible and as freely as necessary. **(15 BE)**

3.2 Summarize the text (Material 3, p. 22) in English in not more than 120 words.

One point (1 BE) will be deducted for every 10 words that you are over the word limit. Please count your words in groups of 10. **(15 BE)**

4 Produktion

Describe the cartoon and interpret the message of the cartoon (Material 4, p. 23) concerning immigration and integration.

Write 270–330 words.

Two points (2 BE) will be deducted for every 15 words that you are over the word limit. Please count your words in groups of 50. **(40 BE)**

Material 1

Young, British and radicalised: Why people want to join Islamic State

In a live debate on Radio 1 we asked what motivates some to head to Syria and Iraq. A small number of British Muslims have joined the notorious Islamic State. It is responsible for
5 mass killings, abductions and beheadings. We also heard the story of Omar, a 27-year-old from High Wycombe in Buckinghamshire, who is now fighting for Islamic State in Syria. [...] He is now on a UN sanctions list set up to
10 tackle terrorism.

BBC Newsnight journalist Secunder Kermani has spent time talking to Omar online.

He says that much of what Omar told him about fighting in battles with IS was "really
15 shocking" – but that Omar was at other times very polite and even "nice".

Omar spoke online about his early life and what set him on a path towards radicalism.

"My childhood was good, nothing out of the
20 ordinary," he explains.

A school friend said Omar "became progressively religious". Omar, like other young jihadis originally from Britain, claims that events following the 9/11 attacks in the US and
25 "unjust Western foreign policy" have been a key motivating force for them. [...]

Rashad Ali, from the Institute of Strategic Dialogue, works with young people attracted to radical ideology. He says the way these
30 people look at the world is to think "everything the West has done is evil and the West is to blame for everything."

In his audio messages, Omar also describes wanting to go to defend the "weak and
35 oppressed women, children and elderly neglected by the West" in the war in Syria. [...]

Omar describes the excitement of making his journey to Syria to do his "Islamic duty" because, he says, he was "leaving the land of immorality and going to a land of jihad." [...] 40

Ismael Lea South, a rapper and activist who converted to Islam, says the crossover with gang culture is clear. "In gangs there is a sense of brotherhood, if you mess with one you mess with all of us," he explains. "Many people who 45 are isolated, going through issues, when they are in a gang they feel a sense of belonging. In Islam we are taught we are all one brotherhood, but certain extremist groups use that to exploit their poison." 50

After 9/11 and then the 7/7 bombings in London, many believe an "us and them mentality" emerged.

"There is greater polarisation between Muslims and non-Muslims in British society," says Alyas 55 Karmani, an imam in Bradford. "There is a sense that young people growing up, the 'war on terror generation', have been exposed to a barrage of Islamophobia in the media, negative portrayals of Muslims." [...] 60

Alyas Karmani describes one 17-year-old he spoke to who had a "totally utopian idea" of Syria being a "promised land" before travelling there to join IS.

Karmani says he told the teenager that "Isis 65 has no legitimacy whatsoever. It cannot claim to be the Islamic State. Scholars have condemned this." [...]

The teenager later died fighting for IS.

(Source: www.bbc.co.uk, 17 November 2015; 501 words)

Material 2

Young people's earning power 'scarred' by older workers staying longer in same job

The earnings prospects of younger people are being scarred permanently because older workers are staying longer in the same job, according to new research. Younger workers
5 are also being hit by a generational divide in which their jobs are more insecure than those of older people, the Resolution Foundation think tank found.

The proportion of young workers in "insecure"
10 work has increased sharply.

Insecurity has risen because a sizeable minority of people are on zero hours contracts, in more insecure self-employment or doing part-time or temporary work when they want
15 to work longer hours.

Paul Gregg, Professor of Economics and Social Policy at the University of Bath and an associate at the foundation, said: "The amount of time people spend in the same job has risen steadily, particularly among women and older workers. 20 But we've also seen people moving between jobs less frequently. This can create a promotion blockage, which in turn hinders young people's career progression and can permanently scar their earnings. Job security is crucial to the 25 pursuit of full employment as it will make work more attractive to those facing the biggest barriers to work. But we should also be mindful about the falling rate of job moves, which are a vital way for young workers to 30 build their careers."

(Source: Andrew Grice, The Independent, 27 July 2015; 226 words)

Material 3

Minderheiten in Großbritannien wenig integriert

Ein für die britische Regierung erstellter Bericht kommt zu dem Schluss, dass ethnische Minderheiten im Königreich zunehmend sozial ausgegrenzt und mangelhaft integriert sind.
5 Das Ausmaß der Isolation sei in einigen Regionen besorgniserregend, schreibt die Verfasserin Dame Louise Casey. Die Politik habe es über Jahrzehnte versäumt, „mit dem beispiellosen Tempo der Einwanderung" Schritt zu hal-
10 ten, heißt es in dem Bericht, der bereits im Juli 2015 vom damaligen Premierminister David Cameron in Auftrag gegeben worden war.

Laut Casey betrifft die Segregation viele Bereiche. So seien ethnische Minderheiten häufig
15 sozial und wirtschaftlich isoliert und würden auf der anderen Seite kulturelle und religiöse Werte vertreten, die den britischen Werten und Gesetzen widersprächen. So würden etwa in einigen Gemeinschaften Frauen ihrer
20 Grundrechte als britische Bürgerinnen beraubt.

Diese Tendenzen seien von der Politik zu lange ignoriert worden. Integrationsarbeit beschränke sich häufig auf „Saris, Samosas und karibische Blechtrommeln", schreibt Casey. Dabei sei 25 es nicht zu verantworten, dass britische Behörden aus Angst vor Rassismusbeschuldigungen umstrittene religiöse Praktiken, sexistisches, frauenfeindliches und patriarchalisches Verhalten ignorierten oder duldeten. 30

Zur Verbesserung der Situation empfiehlt Casey der Regierung die Einführung eines Eids auf britische Werte für Einwanderer, Maßnahmen zu sozialer Durchmischung vor allem junger Menschen, sowie die umfassende Förde- 35 rung der englischen Sprache. In der Verantwortung sieht Casey aber nicht nur die offizielle Seite; auch die Einwanderer müssten mehr Leistungen erbringen. Gerade isolierte muslimische Gemeinden in Orten wie Oldham, 40 Bradford und Birmingham müssten „viel, viel besser in Sachen Integration" werden.

(Source: Die Zeit, 5 December 2016; 241 words)

Material 4

(Source: cartoonstock/Karsten Schley)

MUSTERPRÜFUNG 4

1 Hörverstehen

Listen to the audio file and complete the table with the relevant information in English based on the information you hear.

(15 BE)

British opinion of GM food (2 BE)	
significance of this finding (2 BE)	
types of GM products available in Britain (3 BE)	
purpose of those GM foods (1 BE)	
supporters' opinion of GM food (2 BE)	
people's thoughts on animal cloning (1 BE)	
information about first cloned sheep (1 BE)	
legal status of food from cloned animals (2 BE)	

how this will change when Britain leaves the EU	
(1 BE)	

2 Leseverstehen

Please read the text (Material 1, p. 27) and complete the table below with the relevant information in German. **(15 BE)**

Was beschreibt der Begriff „Parallelleben"? (4 BE)	
Welche Sorge hat der Autor? (1 BE)	
Welche Institution kann dieses Muster brechen? (1 BE)	
Wie soll diese Institution sein? (3 BE)	
Welchem Fach wird mittlerweile weniger Priorität eingeräumt? (1 BE)	
Was sagen Psychologen über eine Gruppe Gleichgesinnter in einem Raum und welche Schlussfolgerung kann man daraus für Schulen ziehen? (3 BE)	

Wie ist die Situation in den Schulen laut Aussage des Autors? (1 BE)	
Wie fühlen sich Mitglieder muslimischer Gemeinden in Birmingham? (1 BE)	

3 Mediation

3.1 Translate the text excerpt (Material 2, p. 27) including the title freely into German. Remember to translate as closely as possible and as freely as necessary. **(15 BE)**

3.2 Summarize the text (Material 3, p. 28) in English in not more than 100 words.

One point (1 BE) will be deducted for every 10 words that you are over the word limit. Please count your words in groups of 10. **(15 BE)**

4 Produktion

What do you think about GM food? Analyse chances and risks you see in buying and consuming GM food.

Altogether write at least 270–330 words.

Two points (2 BE) will be deducted for every 15 words that you are over the word limit. Please count your words in groups of 50. **(40 BE)**

Material 1

Muslim schoolchildren are still leading parallel lives to the mainstream

Thirteen years ago I coined the phrase "parallel lives" to describe the segregation of Asian and white communities in the riot-torn towns of northern England. People from different
5 communities did not live in the same areas, work in the same places, or share social and cultural activities. More importantly, they did not go to school together. My worry is that nothing has changed since my report in 2001.

10 Often schools are the only way to break this pattern of segregation. They should be safe places, in which pupils learn about different faiths and backgrounds, share experiences and develop common bonds. In mixed schools, this
15 may happen naturally as children grow up alongside each other, visiting each other's houses and taking part in shared activities. Without this, the students will emerge into a diverse world ill-equipped "to live and work in
20 a multicultural, multi-faith and democratic Britain" – to use a phrase from the recent "Trojan Horse" Ofsted Reports.

The Labour government attempted to tackle intolerance by imposing a duty on schools "to
25 promote community cohesion". This was imposed on all state schools – faith and non-faith. Unfortunately, the Education Act of 2011 removed the requirement for Ofsted to apply this criterion when inspecting schools.

30 Another mistake has been to downgrade citizenship education, with the Secretary of State giving it less priority in the curriculum.

Psychologists tell us that if we put a group of like-minded people in a room they become
35 more like-minded. In a school environment, the best insurance against this is to make sure teachers are recruited openly, without reference to faith or background and that the pupils come from the widest set of backgrounds.

As I said, the situation has hardly improved 40 since my report. Many monocultural schools remain. With faith schools established for majority faiths, the growing number of applications emerging from minority and less established faiths cannot be denied. There are 45 now Sikh and Hindu faith schools alongside Muslim and Jewish schools.

And Islam is not the only religion with extreme adherents who hold views about women and individual rights that are inimical to our 50 Western, liberal society.

Faith schools also prop up a system of community and faith leaders, giving them real power over their communities – what could be more important to a parent than their gaining 55 admission for their children? Some faith leaders use this power wisely; others use it to build a bigger stronghold.

Muslim communities in Birmingham will no doubt feel that they have been singled out and 60 demonised, and that the judgments are politically motivated and unjustified. Whether or not this is the case, let us hope that out of this mess we can build a new commitment to more inclusive schools and to ensuring that all 65 our children are provided with a broader view of the world. This should be an objective shared by all political parties.

(Source: Ted Cantle, The Daily Telegraph, 11 June 2014; 486 words)

Material 2

Is the typical U.S. family a concept of the past?

In the 1950s a normal family had one breadwinner, normally the father, who went to work in the morning and came back (late) in the evening. The mother stayed at home and took care of the family. A concept that we all 5 know is not seen very often anymore today.

A report published by the Council on Contemporary Families, it is written that in the 1950s 65 percent of all children under 15 lived
10 in a family just like that. Today, this is only true for 22 percent.

Today, many children live in families where both parents work. This is called a dual-income family. But even though this is the most
15 common concept, it only applies for 34 percent of all children. So how do the other children live? Well, almost a quarter of all children are being raised by a single mother. 23 percent, to be precise. But there are also single fathers?
20 True. 3 percent live with a single father. 7 percent of all children live in a family where the father or the mother lives with an unmarried partner (who is not the father/

mother of the child). The remaining 3 percent live with their grandparents. 25

The reasons for this situation are manifold. The economy has changed a lot, people, and especially so women, have higher educations. The job market has become better for women which gives them more opportunities and 30 more independence. There is less gender discrimination and the welfare system has gotten better since the 1960s.

But the biggest truth is that less people are getting married. Whereas in 1950 two-thirds of 35 all households were married couples with children the numbers have declined in 2010 to only 45 percent.

Material 3

Rana Plaza hat wenig verändert

Als vor drei Jahren beim Einsturz einer Textilfabrik in Bangladesch mehr als 1.000 Menschen ums Leben kamen, gelobten die internationalen Modekonzerne Besserung. Schon drei
5 Wochen danach unterzeichneten Gewerkschaften und Branchenvertreter einen Aktionsplan, der besseren Brandschutz und mehr Gebäudesicherheit bringen sollte. Doch seither sind immer wieder Fabrikgebäude in Brand ge-
10 raten oder eingestürzt, und Menschen starben.

Der jüngste Fall ereignete sich am Samstagmorgen vor einer Woche im Industriegebiet Tongi, rund 20 Kilometer nördlich der Hauptstadt Dhaka. Nach einer Explosion brach dort
15 beim Verpackungshersteller Tampaco Foils ein Feuer aus. Es dauerte mehr als 30 Stunden, den Großbrand zu löschen. Die Bilanz, eine Woche danach: 34 Menschen verbrannten, erstickten oder wurden erschlagen. 34 Verletzte befan-
20 den sich zum gleichen Zeitpunkt noch im Krankenhaus.

Menschenrechtler fordern nun, die ausländischen Unternehmen noch stärker in die Pflicht zu nehmen. „Die Realität zeigt, dass der hohe
25 Preisdruck und die Einhaltung der Menschenrechte nicht immer zusammengehen", sagt

Carolijn Terwindt vom European Center for Constitutional and Human Rights (ECCHR). Die Menschenrechtsorganisation Human Rights Watch nennt den Brand von Tongi ein „Déjà 30 Vu". Tatsächlich gab es auch nach Inkrafttreten des Aktionsplans immer wieder Fabrikunglücke in Bangladesch.

Mehr als 200 internationale Auftraggeber aus der Modebranche haben sich bislang im 35 Aktionsplan für Brandschutz und Gebäudesicherheit zusammengeschlossen. Sie wollen nur noch in Fabriken produzieren lassen, die sie mit eigenen Inspektoren vor Ort überprüft haben. 40

Was den Brand in Tongi ausgelöst hat, ist auch eine Woche nach dem Unglück noch nicht klar. Womöglich gab es ein Leck in einer Gasleitung. Den örtlichen Behörden zufolge hat der Fabrikbesitzer nur zwei Tage vor dem Unfall rund 20 45 Tonnen leicht entflammbare Chemikalien ins Werk gebracht. Ob sie dort entsprechend der Sicherheitsvorschriften gelagert wurden, wisse man noch nicht.

(Source: Die Zeit, 18 September 2016; 283 words)

Training

Teil A Hörverstehen

Für diese Aufgabe hören Sie einen Text, der zwischen 3 und 6 Minuten dauert. Sie müssen hier Ihr Hörverständnis beweisen. Dieses Hörverständnis wird durch verschiedene Aufgabenformate überprüft. Beim Hörverstehen können folgende Aufgabenformate vorkommen:

- Ausfüllen einer Tabelle, Übersicht oder eines Formulars mit kurzen Informationen oder Stichpunkten
- Wiedergabe der Hauptpunkte des Hörtextes auf Deutsch oder Englisch
- Beantwortung von Fragen auf Deutsch oder Englisch
- Vervollständigen von Teilsätzen
- *Multiple-Choice*-Aufgaben
- Zuordnungsaufgaben

Beim Hörverstehen können Sie maximal 15 Punkte erreichen.

Lesen Sie sich vor dem Hören die Aufgabenstellung genau durch. Dazu gehört auch, dass Sie sich die Fragen oder Hauptpunkte, zu denen Sie Inhalte im Text heraushören sollen, genau durchlesen. So können Sie beim Hören Wichtiges von Unwichtigem unterscheiden. Normalerweise werden Inhalte chronologisch abgefragt. Das bedeutet, dass Inhalte zu einer Frage am Anfang Ihres Aufgabenblattes am Anfang des Hörtextes genannt werden und zu den letzten Fragen dann auch am Ende des Hörtextes Informationen gegeben werden.

Wichtig ist außerdem: Es ist nicht schlimm, wenn Sie nicht jedes einzelne Wort verstehen! Wichtig ist, den Text als Ganzes bzw. das für die Aufgaben Relevante zu verstehen. Halten Sie sich nicht an einem Wort auf, das Sie nicht kennen. Solange Sie darüber nachdenken, was ein bestimmtes Wort wohl heißen könnte, bekommen Sie ganz viel, von dem was nun in der Folge gesagt wird, nicht mehr mit. Daher bietet es sich auch an, einfach auf Englisch mitzuskribbeln, selbst wenn die Aufgabe auf Deutsch zu bearbeiten ist. Rechtschreibung und Grammatik sind beim Notizen machen unwichtig und Sie kommen nicht in Versuchung, durch Übersetzungsversuche vom Zuhören abgelenkt zu werden. Für eine deutsche Übersetzung und ‚Reinschrift' ist auch nach dem Hören noch ausreichend Zeit.

So verbessern Sie Ihr Hörverstehen:

- Hören Sie englische Hörbücher oder andere, kürzere Texte, die Sie im Internet finden. Überall im Internet gibt es englische Podcasts.
- Schauen Sie Filme auf Englisch an. Zwar erleichtert hier das Sehen auch das Hörverstehen, aber das macht nichts. Versuchen Sie, so gut es geht, auf Untertitel zu verzichten, denn sonst schulen Sie Ihr Leseverstehen.
- Schauen Sie britische und amerikanische Fernsehsender, z. B. CNN oder BBC World.

Hörtext 1: Grundlagen schaffen

Am wichtigsten ist es zu erkennen, worum es in dem Hörtext geht. Hören Sie sich den Hörtext an (es handelt sich lediglich um die ersten 30 Sekunden eines längeren Texts) und beantworten Sie folgende Fragen:

1 Das Thema des Hörtextes ist: _____

2 Die Anzahl der Sprecher beträgt: _____

3 Die Textsorte ist (bitte ankreuzen):

A ☐   ein Interview

B ☐   ein Monolog

C ☐   ein Gespräch

4 Die Stimmung ist (bitte ankreuzen):

A ☐   freundlich

B ☐   angespannt

C ☐   neutral

🎧 Hörtext 2: Eine Tabelle vervollständigen
006-008

Die fünf kurzen Hörtexte bestehen aus einzelnen Aussagen zum Thema Globalisierung und sind Monologe. Normalerweise werden in der Prüfung Informationen in einer Tabelle in einer Sprache gefordert; in dieser Übung werden Sie aber das Aufschreiben der Informationen jeweils auf Deutsch und Englisch üben.

Übung 1: Informationen entnehmen und auf Deutsch notieren

Hören Sie den ersten beiden Sprechern zu und vervollständigen Sie die Tabelle mit Informationen zu den Themen, die in der Tabelle erwähnt sind.

Was ist Globalisierung?	
der Grund für Globalisierung	
Globalisierung und Kultur	

1 Hören Sie nur dem ersten Sprecher zu. Welche dieser Wörter hören Sie? Kreisen Sie sie ein.

> globalization – integration – international economy – national economies –
> single global economy – transport – global communications – infrastructure – huge growth –
> cross-border trade and investment

2 Übersetzen Sie die eingekreisten Wörter.

_____

_____

_____

3   Notieren Sie in Ihren eigenen Worten, was Globalisierung ist und warum sie entstanden ist. Tragen Sie Ihr Ergebnis in die ersten beiden Zeilen der Tabelle auf S. 30 ein.

4   Hören Sie nun den Beitrag der zweiten Sprecherin. Welche dieser Wörter hören Sie? Kreisen Sie sie ein.

> cultural integration – access to information – satellite television – newspapers – fake news – the internet – ideas can spread – American-style food – American values – the English language – democracy – the western lifestyle

5   Übersetzen Sie die eingekreisten Wörter.

_____

_____

_____

6   Notieren Sie in Ihren eigenen Worten, was zum Thema Globalisierung und Kultur gesagt wird. Tragen Sie Ihr Ergebnis in die dritte Zeile der Tabelle auf S. 30 ein.

7   Hören Sie nun die beiden Beiträge noch einmal und überprüfen Sie Ihre Lösungen auf Richtigkeit. Nehmen Sie gegebenenfalls Verbesserungen, Änderungen und Ergänzungen vor.

Übung 2: Informationen entnehmen und auf Englisch notieren

Listen to the third speaker and complete the table with the relevant information in English based on the information you hear.

people and jobs	

1   Was ist das Thema? Kreuzen Sie die richtige Lösung an:

A ☐   outsourcing of jobs

B ☐   cultural consequences of globalization

C ☐   the growing economies of Asia

2   Hören Sie dem Sprecher ein zweites Mal zu. Kreisen Sie die Wörter im Kasten ein, die Sie hören.

> destruction – clothing industry – textiles – production – fewer jobs in factories – jobs are being outsourced – companies outsource production – automation – living off benefits – dead-end jobs – society divided – no future

3   Hören Sie dem Sprecher nun ein drittes Mal zu. Tragen Sie die geforderten Informationen in die Tabelle ein.

Übung 3: Die restliche Tabelle ausfüllen

Listen to the fourth and fifth speakers and complete the table with the relevant information. The information taken from the remarks of the fourth speaker must be in German, the information taken from the remarks of the fifth speaker in English.

Sprecherin 4: Ziele des Sprechens über Globalisierung	
Speaker 5: consequences of globalization	

Hörtext 3: Beantworten von Fragen auf Deutsch oder auf Englisch

Übung 1: Fragen auf Englisch beantworten

Sie müssen die Antwort nicht wortwörtlich aus dem Hörtext aufschreiben. Wichtig ist, dass Sie die Inhalte sinngemäß wiedergeben, d. h. Sie dürfen notfalls Wörter ändern.

Hören Sie den Text und beantworten Sie die Fragen auf Englisch.

1   How has the concentration of carbon dioxide changed in recent years?

_____

2   Who is responsible for the changing climate and why?

_____

Zu Frage 1: Die Frage lesen.

1   Auf welche Wörter in Frage 1 müssen Sie beim Hören achten?

_____

2   Welches Verb und welches Zeitadverb kommen in der Aufgabe vor?

_____

3   Achten Sie auf die Zeitform des Verbs. In welcher Zeitform müssen Sie antworten?

_____

Zu Frage 1: Dem Hörtext zuhören.

1 Welche Zeitadverbien kommen im relevanten Satz des Hörtexts vor?

_____

2 Welches Verb kommt im relevanten Satz des Hörtexts vor?

_____

Zu Frage 1: Die Antwort schreiben.

Da die Zeitform in Frage 1 eine andere als die im Hörtext ist, entscheiden Sie, welche der folgenden Verben am geeignetsten für die Antwort ist:

A ☐ has increased

B ☐ is higher

C ☐ has become higher

D ☐ has got higher

Schreiben Sie nun Ihre Antwort zu Frage 1 auf S. 32.

Zu Frage 2: Die Frage lesen.

1 Auf welche Wörter in der Frage müssen Sie beim Hören achten?

_____

2 Wenn ein _why_ in der Frage vorkommt, welches englisches Wort muss in der Antwort vorkommen?

_____

Zu Frage 2: Dem Hörtext zuhören.

1 Wer verursacht den Klimawandel?

_____

2 Wie wird das Klima verändert?

_____

Zu Frage 2: Die Antwort schreiben.

Vervollständigen Sie die beiden Lücken:

_____ are responsible for the changing climate, because _____

_____

Schreiben Sie nun die ganze Antwort zu Frage 2 auf S. 32.

Übung 2: Fragen auf Deutsch beantworten

Hier müssen Sie die englische Aussage des Hörtexts aufschreiben und ins Deutsche übersetzen.

Hören Sie den Text und beantworten Sie die Fragen auf Deutsch.

1 Warum können wir nicht warten, bis wir etwas gegen Erderwärmung unternehmen?

_____

_____

2 Welche Konsequenzen hat der Klimawandel für Großbritannien?

_____

_____

_____

Frage 1

1 Welcher dieser Ausdrücke im Hörtext kommt dem Wort „warten" am nächsten:

A ☐ must decline

B ☐ avoid

C ☐ putting off action

D ☐ reduce

2 Listen Sie die drei Folgen des Wartens auf Englisch auf:

1 _____

2 _____

3 _____

3 Übersetzen Sie die Folgen und schreiben Sie die Antwort zu Frage 1 oben.

Frage 2

1 Welche dieser Wörter hören Sie im relevanten Teil des Texts? Übersetzen die im Hörtext vorhandenen Wörter auf Deutsch.

A ☐ warmer winters _____

B ☐ rainy summer _____

C ☐ uncomfortably hot in the summer _____

D ☐ hot and sweaty temperatures _____

E ☐ less predictable _____

F ☐ more frequent extreme weather like storms and floods

_____

G ☐ comfortable weather _____

2 Schreiben Sie nun die Antwort zu Frage 2 auf S. 34 in einem Satz. Achten Sie auf stilistisch gutes und grammatikalisch richtiges Deutsch.

🎧 Hörtext 4: Verschiedene Aufgaben
010

Mit diesem Text üben Sie nun drei verschiedene Aufgabenformate.

Übung 1: *Multiple-Choice*-Aufgaben

Alle Aufgaben beziehen sich auf die erste Hälfte des Textes.

1 Tick the correct answer according to the audio text.

Gerardo was deported to Mexico …

A ☐ six weeks ago.

B ☐ six months ago.

C ☐ just now.

Schreiben Sie die Wörter aus dem Hörtext auf, die Ihre Antwort unterstützen:

_____

2 Tick the correct answer according to the audio text.

Julio's father was deported because …

A ☐ he arrived in the USA illegally.

B ☐ he parked illegally.

C ☐ Donald Trump does not like Mexicans.

Zwei der Aussagen befinden sich im Text. Welche? Notieren Sie die Wörter aus dem Text.

1 _____

2 _____

Welche der beiden Aussagen wird in den Zusammenhang mit der Abschiebung gemacht?

_____

3 Tick the correct answer according to the audio text.

Every time Eva sees her father ...

A ☐   she becomes emotional.

B ☐   she finds it stressful.

C ☐   she gets scared.

Alle drei Emotionen kommen im Text vor, aber in welchem Zusammenhang? Ordnen Sie Satzbausteine einander zu, indem Sie die Buchstaben in die jeweiligen Kästchen unten schreiben. (Es gibt einen Halbsatz zu viel.)

1 The journey to see her dad is ...   ☐   A   emotional

2 When she heard the sirens, she felt ...   ☐   B   stressful

3 Eva's mum is highly ...   ☐   C   scared

4 Seeing her dad makes her ...   ☐

Nun kreuzen Sie das richtige Kästchen in Aufgabe 3 oben an.

4 Tick the correct answer according to the audio text.

Julio's dad lives near the border because ...

A ☐   he got a good job there.

B ☐   the Americans deported him there.

C ☐   he wants to be near his family.

A   ist nicht richtig, weil im Text steht: "He's got a job but _____."

B   ist nicht richtig, weil im Text steht, dass er nach Mexico City deportiert wurde und "Mexico City

is _____ from San Diego."

Übung 2: Einen Satz vervollständigen

Vervollständigen Sie die folgenden Sätze. Alle Lösungen befinden sich im zweiten Teil des Hörtextes.

1 Complete the sentence below.

The mother's new role in the family is _____ .

Was sagt die Mutter über sich selbst, jetzt, wo ihr Mann nicht mehr bei der Familie lebt?
(3 Aspekte)

1 _____

2 _____

3 _____

Welche Aussage beschreibt ihre neue Rolle?

1 ☐ 2 ☐ 3 ☐

Nun vervollständigen Sie Satz 1 auf S. 36.

2 Complete the sentence below.

One possibility for the future is that they all _____ .

1 Welches Wort im Text könnte durch *possibility* ersetzt werden:

A ☐ option

B ☐ hope

C ☐ routine

2 Wer verwendet das Wort und welche Lösung für die getrennte Familie erwähnt er/sie (auf Deutsch)?

_____

Vervollständigen Sie nun Satz 2 oben.

3 Complete the sentence below.

Two things Eva misses are _____ and _____ .

Welche der folgenden Dinge erwähnt Eva in Ihrer Aussage gegen Ende des Hörtextes:

A ☐ daily calls

B ☐ going to church

C ☐ hugs

D ☐ breakfast before school

E ☐ holidays

F ☐ her future

G ☐ advice from her father

H ☐ college

I ☐ career

2 Welche Dinge in dieser Liste vermisst Eva?

_____

Vervollständigen Sie nun Satz 3 oben.

Übung 3: Aussagen zuordnen

Listen to the audio text and match the speakers to the statements. There are two more statements than needed.

A	Gerardo
B	presenter
C	Eva
D	Julio
E	Fernanda

1	Our whole lives are about separation.
2	Our dad worries about us a lot.
3	Life has become hard for our mum.
4	I still talk to Gerardo about everyday things.
5	I feel that the children have lost both their parents.
6	We're not the only family that moves between Mexico and the USA.
7	There are hundreds of kids in the USA who have had one parent deported.

Vergessen Sie nicht, dass die Aussagen immer chronologisch im Hörtext zu hören sind.

1 Einen Namen kann man ausschließen, da über diese Person nur gesprochen wird. Über welche Person wird im Text nur gesprochen, ohne dass sie selbst spricht?

_____

2 Schreiben Sie die Stichwörter in jeder Aussage auf, auf die man beim Hören achten muss:

1 _____

2 _____

3 _____

4 _____

5 _____

6 _____

3 Achten Sie beim zweiten Hören darauf, wer die Aussage macht. Bedenken Sie, dass zwei Aussagen nicht zutreffen und daher nicht im Text vorkommen. Schreiben Sie die richtigen Namen zur jeweiligen Aussage unten in die Tabelle und notieren Sie welche Aussagen im Hörtext nicht vorkommen.

1	
2	
3	
4	
5	
6	
7	

Teil B Leseverstehen

Für diese Aufgabe bekommen Sie einen Text, der zwischen 300 und 500 Wörtern lang ist. Sie müssen hier Ihr Textverständnis beweisen. Dieses Textverständnis kann durch verschiedene Aufgabenformate überprüft werden.

Beim Leseverstehen können Sie maximal 15 Punkte erreichen. Nehmen Sie sich ungefähr 45 Minuten Zeit, um diese Aufgabe zu bearbeiten. Nehmen Sie die Aufgabe nicht zu leicht. Überfliegen Sie den Text nicht nur oberflächlich, sondern lassen Sie sich Zeit für eine genaue Lektüre.

Lesen Sie den Text mehrmals aufmerksam durch. Schlagen Sie die – und nur die – Vokabeln nach, die Sie für das Textverständnis unbedingt brauchen. Sie müssen nicht jedes einzelne Wort des Textes verstehen.

Lesen Sie auch die Aufgabenstellung genau durch. Stellen Sie sicher, dass Sie diese genau verstehen. Nichts ist ärgerlicher, als die Aufgabenstellung nur zu überfliegen und dann die Aufgaben falsch zu bearbeiten, obwohl Sie sie mit etwas mehr Zeit und Muße richtig verstanden hätten.

1 Multiple Choice

Bei dieser Aufgabenart sollten Sie den Text besonders genau lesen, denn manchmal kann die Tücke im Detail liegen. Legen Sie besonderes Augenmerk auf die „kleinen Wörter", also Adjektive und Adverbien. Diese ändern eine Aussage oft massiv, auch wenn sie noch so unwichtig anmuten. Lassen Sie sich von augenscheinlich ähnlichen Auswahlmöglichkeiten nicht aufs Glatteis führen. Sie können davon ausgehen, dass die Fragen chronologisch den Text entlang gehen. Suchen Sie also die Antwort auf eine der ersten Fragen nicht am Ende des Textes und umgekehrt.

Robin Hood's Sherwood Forest faces fracking threat

The latest battleground for the future of fracking in Britain looks set to be Sherwood Forest, the legendary home of folk hero Robin Hood and now the target of a seismic survey by Ineos.

The chemical multinational, which relocated its headquarters back to the UK last month, appears to have agreed terms with the Forestry Commission to start burying charges and spend up to two years using "thumper trucks" or vibroseis machines to search for shale gas.

Campaigners have called on the government to block any possible fracking and protect the forest.

According to documents obtained under freedom of information request by Friends of the Earth, Ineos could be working within 200 metres of the Major Oak, a 1,000-year old tree that in folklore sheltered Robin Hood and his merry men.

Commercial fracking has yet to start in Britain, although Ineos and other firms have obtained licences from the government for shale gas exploration. The technology has been deeply controversial since tests conducted by Cuadrilla in 2011 caused earth tremors near Blackpool, but fracking operations are expected to restart in five wells in Yorkshire and Lancashire later this year.

A small protest camp has been established at Kirby Misperton, North Yorkshire, at one of the wells where gas firm Third Energy has been given permission to start fracking.

Guy Shrubsole, a Friends of the Earth campaigner, said he expected the move to search for shale gas under Sherwood Forest to become a new rallying point. He said: "I can't think of anything more iconic in the English mindset to go for. You'd have thought they'd have learnt from the mistakes of some of the other fracking companies to avoid it, but they've gone straight for it."

Ineos told the Daily Telegraph that no decision had been made on whether fracking would go ahead under the national nature reserve, adding that "any decision to position a well site will take into account environmental features such as the Major Oak".

The firm's shale operations director, Tom
50 Pickering, said: "Potentially we in the UK have
a huge supply of indigenous gas under our
own feet. It would be simply crazy not to
explore this natural resource."

However, Friends of the Earth fear that the
55 seismic surveys alone could damage the forest,
whose core is a site of special scientific interest,
and its wildlife, which include rare bats and
other protected species as well as ancient
woodland.

*(Source: Gwyn Topham, Guardian, 1 January 2017;
410 words)*

Übung 1: Genau lesen

1 Why do campaigners want to stop fracking in Sherwood Forest? Tick the correct answer according
to the text.

A ☐ Because they agree with the Forestry Commission that fracking is bad for the environment.

B ☐ Because they are worried about the impact on a legendary forest and in particular a
famous old tree.

C ☐ Because Major Oak will be destroyed.

D ☐ Because they fear that tourists who want to see where Robin Hood lived won't come to
visit anymore.

Schauen Sie sich die obige Aufgabe an und vergleichen Sie die Antwortmöglichkeiten mit dem Text.
Entscheiden Sie dann, welche Aufgabe richtig ist.

A In welchem Textabschnitt vermuten Sie die Antwort auf die Frage?

Schreiben Sie die Zeilennummern auf: _____

B Schauen Sie Aussage **1A** an: Was steht über die *Forestry Commission* im Text?
Kreuzen Sie an:

☐ Sie sind für *fracking*. ☐ Sie sind gegen *fracking*.

C Schauen Sie Aussage **1B** an: Wie weit entfernt von dem berühmten Baum werden die Arbeiten

stattfinden? _____

D Schauen Sie Aussage **1C** an: Welche Informationen gibt es im Text zu Major Oak?

_____

E Schauen Sie Aussage **1D** an: Welche Aussage bezogen auf Robin Hood wird im Text gemacht?

_____

Was steht im Text über Tourismus? _____

_____

F   Entscheiden Sie nun, welche der vier Aussagen die richtige Antwort auf die Frage ist, kreuzen Sie das richtige Feld an (S. 40), und erklären Sie, warum.

_____

_____

Übung 2: Genau lesen

2   How is fracking viewed in general? Tick the correct answer according to the text.

A ☐   It is widely accepted as being good for the country, which is why there will be five more wells.

B ☐   Everybody is excited about the future of fracking.

C ☐   It has caused a lot of angry public discussion and disagreement, but only a view are protesting against it.

D ☐   The technology has been examined in depth, so people feel it is safe.

A   In welchem Textabschnitt vermuten Sie die Antwort auf die Frage?

Schreiben Sie die Zeilennummern auf: _____

B   Schauen Sie Aussage **2 A** an: Eine der beiden Teilaussagen steht nicht im Text. Welche? Kreuzen Sie an.

☐ die erste   ☐ die zweite

C   Schauen Sie Aussage **2 B** an: Was bedeutet das Adjektiv *excited* i. d. R. auf Deutsch?

_____

Steht eine Aussage im Text, die mit *excited* zu tun hat?

☐ ja ☐ nein

D   Schauen Sie Aussage **2 C** an: Schlagen Sie das Wort *controversial* nach und entscheiden Sie, ob die Bedeutung dieses Wortes zum Sachverhalt der Aussage passt.

☐ ja ☐ nein

Wieviel Leute protestieren?

_____

E   Schauen Sie Aussage **2 D** an: Finden Sie Informationen zu der ersten Aussage „The technology has been examined in depth" im Text?

☐ ja ☐ nein

Finden Sie Informationen zu der zweiten Aussage „people feel it is safe" in der relevanten Passage?

☐ ja ☐ nein

F   Entscheiden Sie nun, welche der vier Aussagen die richtige Antwort auf die Frage ist, kreuzen Sie das richtige Feld an, und erklären Sie warum.

_____

_____

Übung 3: Selbstständig arbeiten

Gehen Sie nun bei der nächsten Aufgabe genauso gründlich vor und erklären Sie, wie Sie zur Lösung gekommen sind.

What is the situation concerning underground shale gas in the UK? Tick the correct box according to the text.

A ☐ Resources are limited and so the country needs to find new sources soon

B ☐ There is an enormous amount of gas just waiting to be found.

C ☐ There is shale gas but it is not known if there is a lot of gas.

D ☐ Finding gas is an expensive and complicated procedure.

_____

_____

_____

_____

_____

_____

_____

_____

2 Ausfüllen einer Tabelle

Bei dieser Aufgabe kommt es darauf an, dass Sie in der Lage sind wichtige Informationen von unwichtigen zu trennen. Extrahieren Sie nur das aus dem Text, was auch in den einzelnen Spalten der Tabelle gefordert ist. Die Aufgabe kann entweder auf Englisch oder auf Deutsch zu bearbeiten sein. Sie müssen entweder konkrete Fragen beantworten oder Informationen zum Text anhand von gegebenen Stichworten finden.

Hierfür bietet es sich an, den Text mit farbigen Stiften zu lesen. Nehmen Sie für jede Spalte eine Farbe und markieren Sie die relevanten Stellen im Text. Achten Sie hierbei auf Schlüsselwörter. Sie sollten vermeiden, dass der Text am Ende komplett farbig ist. Haben Sie Mut, Dinge unmarkiert zu lassen.

The War on Coal is over!

"This is what this is all about," Trump said today at the Environmental Protection Agency headquarters. "Bringing back our jobs, bringing back our dreams and making America wealthy
5 again."

[...] As part of the roll-back, Trump will initiate a review of the Clean Power Plan, which restricts greenhouse gas emissions at coal-fired power plants. The regulation [...] has been the subject of long-running legal challenges by 10 Republican-led states and those who profit from burning oil, coal and gas.

Trump, who has called global warming a 'hoax' invented by the Chinese, has repeatedly criticized the power-plant rule and others as 15 an attack on American workers and the struggling US coal industry.

[…] Trump repeated that point saying, "We're going to have safety, we're going to have clean
20 water, we're going to have clean air, but so many [regulations] are unnecessary and so many are job-killing."

[…] In addition to pulling back from the Clean Power Plan, the administration will also lift a
25 14-month-old moratorium on new coal leases on federal lands. […] Trump accused his predecessor of waging a "War on Coal" and boasted in a speech to Congress that he has made "a historic effort to massively reduce
30 job-crushing regulations," including some that threaten "the future and livelihoods of our great coal miners". […] The administration is still in discussion about whether it intends to withdraw from the Paris Agreement on
35 climate change. But the moves to be announced Tuesday will undoubtedly make it more difficult for the US to achieve its goals. […] The overwhelming majority of studies and climate scientists agree the planet is
40 warming, mostly due to man-made sources, including carbon dioxide, methane, halocarbons and nitrogen oxide. The official who briefed reporters said the president does believe in man-made climate change. […]
45 Renewable energy – including wind, solar and biofuels – now accounts for more than 650,000 US jobs.

The Obama administration, some Democratic-led states and environmental groups countered that it will spur thousands of clean-energy jobs and help the US meet ambitious goals to 50 reduce carbon pollution set by the international agreement signed in Paris. […] According to an Energy Department analysis released in January, coal mining now accounts for fewer than 70,000 US jobs. […] Former Vice President 55 Al Gore, who met with Trump at Trump Tower during the transition, called the president's move today a "misguided step away from a sustainable, carbon-free future for ourselves and generations to come." Gore called on the 60 U.S. to continue to be a leader in the climate change fight, saying it's an imperative for both the environment and the economy.

"No matter how discouraging this executive order may be, we must, we can and we will 65 solve the climate crisis,' Gore said. 'No one man or one group can stop the encouraging and escalating momentum we are experiencing in fight to protect our planet."

(Source: Nikki Schwab et al, The Daily Mail, 28 March 2017; 494 words)

Übung 1: Ausfüllen einer Tabelle mit Informationen auf Englisch

Read the text and complete the table below with the relevant information in English.

	Information from the text
changes President Trump initiated	
consequences of those changes	

A Lesen Sie sich die Information in der Tabelle durch und markieren Sie die Schlüsselwörter mit je einer Farbe pro Zeile.

B Lesen Sie den relevanten Auszug aus dem Text (S. 44) erneut aufmerksam durch. Nehmen Sie dieselben Farben wie in Aufgabe **A** und markieren Sie alles, was Sie zu den Schlüsselwörtern im Text finden.

"This is what this is all about," Trump said today at the Environmental Protection Agency headquarters. "Bringing back our jobs, bringing back our dreams and making America wealthy
5 again."

[...] As part of the roll-back, Trump will initiate a review of the Clean Power Plan, which restricts greenhouse gas emissions at coal-fired power plants. The regulation [...] has been
10 the subject of long-running legal challenges by Republican-led states and those who profit from burning oil, coal and gas.

Trump, who has called global warming a 'hoax' invented by the Chinese, has repeatedly
15 criticized the power-plant rule and others as an attack on American workers and the struggling US coal industry.

[...] Trump repeated that point saying, "We're going to have safety, we're going to have clean water, we're going to have clean air, but so 20 many [regulations] are unnecessary and so many are job-killing."

[...] In addition to pulling back from the Clean Power Plan, the administration will also lift a 14-month-old moratorium on new coal leases 25 on federal lands. [...] Trump accused his predecessor of waging a "War on Coal" and boasted in a speech to Congress that he has made "a historic effort to massively reduce job-crushing regulations," including some that 30 threaten "the future and livelihoods of our great coal miners".

C   Schreiben Sie nun auf Englisch in die Tabelle auf S. 43, was Sie im Text gefunden haben.

Übung 2: Ausfüllen einer Tabelle mit Informationen auf Deutsch

Read the text and complete the table below with relevant information from the text in German.

	Informationen aus dem Text
Wie kommentiert Trump den Zustand der Umwelt?	
Wie sieht die Opposition die Folgen der Veränderungen?	

A   Lesen Sie sich die Aufgaben in der Tabelle durch und markieren Sie die Schlüsselwörter mit je einer Farbe pro Zeile.

B   Lesen Sie nun den relevanten Auszug aus dem Text erneut (S. 45) aufmerksam durch. Nehmen Sie dieselben Farben wie in Aufgabe **A**. und markieren Sie alles, was Sie zu den Schlüsselwörtern im Text finden.

Trump, who has called global warming a 'hoax' invented by the Chinese, has repeatedly criticized the power-plant rule and others as an attack on American workers and the
5 struggling US coal industry. [...]

The Obama administration, some Democratic-led states and environmental groups countered that it will spur thousands of clean-energy jobs and help the US meet ambitious goals to
10 reduce carbon pollution set by the international agreement signed in Paris. [...] According to an Energy Department analysis released in January, coal mining now accounts for fewer than 70,000 US jobs. [...] Former Vice President Al Gore, who met with Trump at Trump Tower 15 during the transition, called the president's move today a "misguided step away from a sustainable, carbon-free future for ourselves and generations to come." [...]

C Schlagen Sie die Wörter nach, die Sie für Ihre Antwort brauchen, aber vielleicht nicht verstehen. Ein paar Wörter sind im Textauszug bereits unterstrichen. Schreiben Sie die deutschen Übersetzungen in die Tabelle.

Englisch	Deutsch
hoax struggling spur account for misguided sustainable	

D Schreiben Sie nun in eigenen Worten auf Deutsch die Informationen aus dem Text zu den jeweiligen Aufgaben in der Tabelle auf S. 44.

3 Sätze vervollständigen

Wichtig bei dieser Aufgabe ist, dass der Satz grammatikalisch richtig fortgesetzt wird. Achten Sie daher ganz besonders auf die Struktur und den Satzbau des Satzanfangs.

Internet addiction 'should be recognised as a clinical disorder', psychiatrist claims

Internet addiction is a serious public health problem and should be officially recognised as a clinical disorder, a psychiatrist claims.

Dr Jerald Block says there are four main telltale
5 symptoms which include: Losing all track of time or neglecting basics such as eating or sleeping; cravings and feelings of withdrawal, including anger, tension or depression, when a computer cannot be accessed; an increased need
10 for better computer equipment and software; and negative effects such as arguments, lying, fatigue, social isolation and poor achievement.

Dr Block claims too many hours spent online gaming, viewing porn or emailing can cause a compulsive-impulsive disorder. Unfortunately, 15 internet addiction is resistant to treatment, entails significant risks and has high relapse rates.

British psychiatrists have previously reported in the journal Advances in Psychiatric 20 Treatment that a "significant minority" – some estimate between five and 10 per cent of online users – are internet addicts. While early research suggested that most are highly

25 educated, introverted men, more recent studies suggest the main problem is among middle-aged women on home computers. Dr Block referred to research on internet addiction in South Korea, which has the highest broadband 30 use worldwide. Ten people died from blood clots from staying seated for too long in internet cafes. A 24-year-old man died after playing an online video game for 86 hours straight and another was murdered in a row 35 over an online game. The government there now considers internet addiction one of its most serious public health issues. It estimates that 210,000 children are affected and need treatment, of whom 80 per cent might need drugs targeting the brain and a quarter could 40 need to be hospitalised. The average South Korean high school student spends about 23 hours per week gaming. Another 1.2 million are believed to be at risk of addiction and in need of counseling. There has been alarm over the 45 soaring numbers of pupils dropping out of school or quitting their jobs to spend more time on computers. Similarly, in China 13.7 per cent of teenagers – around 10 million – are reported to be internet addicts. 50

(Source: The Daily Mail, 23 March 2008; 361 words)

Read the text and complete the sentences below.

1 One of the symptoms of internet addiction is not doing basic everyday essential things like

_____ .

2 It used to be thought that internet addicts were mostly _____

_____

but new research shows that actually _____

_____

who are more likely to be addicted to the internet.

3 There have been cases of people dying from thrombosis because they _____

_____

4 In South Korea there are worries about the large number of pupils who _____

_____ and people who _____

_____

Finden Sie die für die vier Sätze relevanten Passagen im Text. Beantworten Sie dazu folgende Fragen:

1 (Satz 1) Im Text werden vier Symptome von Internetsucht aufgelistet. Bei welchem Symptom werden alltägliche Aktivitäten erwähnt?

_____

_____

2 Welche zwei Personengruppen werden möglicherweise durch Internetsucht gefährdet?

A _____

B _____

Welche Gruppe ist bereits in früheren Studien als internetsüchtig aufgefallen?

A ☐   **B** ☐

3 Was ist eine *thrombosis*? Wo im Text steht ein anderer Begriff dafür?

_____

4 Finden Sie andere Wörter/Ausdrücke im Text für *worries*:

worries: _____

Nun vervollständigen Sie die Sätze auf S. 46 mit Ausdrucken aus dem Text. Sie sollten nach Möglichkeit Wörter aus dem Text übernehmen aber möglicherweise müssen Sie sie grammatikalisch anpassen (z. B. ein Gerundium in ein Verb umwandeln).

Teil C Mediation und Übersetzung (Translation)

In dieser Aufgabe müssen Sie zuerst einen englischsprachigen Text ins Deutsche übersetzen und dann einen deutschsprachigen Text ins Englische übertragen.

Der zu übersetzende englischsprachige Text umfasst ca. 150 Wörter. Bei der Übersetzung des englischen Textes ins Deutsche sollten Sie getreu dem Motto „So genau wie möglich, so frei wie nötig" arbeiten.

Der zu übertragende deutschsprachige Text umfasst 200–300 Wörter. Bei der Mediation ins Englische soll eine Zusammenfassung (*summary*) auf Englisch erstellt werden. Hier können Sie freier vorgehen.

Für die Bewältigung beider Aufgaben sollten Sie ungefähr insgesamt 45 Minuten einplanen. Sie können maximal 15 Punkte pro Text erreichen.

Zur Lösung beider Prüfungsaufgaben werden Sie wahrscheinlich vom zugelassenen zweisprachigen Klausurwörterbuch besonders profitieren.

Was ist eine Mediation?

Mediation bedeutet „Vermittlung". In einer solchen Aufgabe entnehmen Sie dem Text Informationen und formulieren diese so, dass jemand, der die Ausgangssprache des Textes nicht beherrscht, einen Überblick über den Text bekommt. Sprachmittlung wird häufig sowohl in der privaten als auch beruflichen Kommunikation angewendet.

Worin besteht der Unterschied zwischen einer Mediation und einer Übersetzung?

Eine *Übersetzung* sollte sehr nah am Text sein. Der Übersetzer hat also in Bezug auf Wortwahl, Satzbau und Struktur wenige Freiheiten. Auch der Stil des Textes sollte erhalten bleiben.

Bei einer *Mediation* darf man sich vom Text weiter entfernen. Oft hat eine Mediationsaufgabe auch die Zusatzaufgabe, den Text für eine bestimmte Person zu übertragen (= adressatengerecht) oder nur bestimmte Teile des Textes zu übertragen. In diesem Fall muss man in der Lage sein, das Wichtige vom Unwichtigen zu trennen. Eine Mediationsaufgabe kann sein – und das ist auch in Ihrer Prüfung so –, einen Text in der anderen Sprache zusammenzufassen. Hier ist es wichtig, dass die Mediation deutlich kürzer als der Originaltext ausfällt. In Ihrer Abschlussprüfung müssen Sie den Text, den Sie auf Englisch zusammenfassen sollen, auf 120 Wörter kürzen. (Manchmal werden aber auch 100 Wörter verlangt.) Achten Sie darauf, diese Wortanzahl nicht zu überschreiten, denn sonst bekommen Sie Punktabzug.

Wie trenne ich das Wichtige vom Unwichtigen, oder: Was sind unwichtige Textstellen?

Oftmals werden in Texten Informationen in Form von direkter Rede oder erläuternden Beispielen wiederholt. Diese Textpassagen können Sie getrost streichen.

Aber Achtung: Es kann das stilistische Merkmal eines Textes sein, die wichtigen Informationen gerade in der direkten Rede zu nennen. Streichen Sie also nicht automatisch diese Passagen heraus, sondern schauen Sie den Text zunächst aufmerksam an und finden Sie heraus, wo die wichtigen Informationen stehen.

Schritt für Schritt zur Übersetzung

1. Lesen Sie den Text mehrmals aufmerksam durch.

2. Unterstreichen Sie die Wörter, die Sie nicht verstehen, und schlagen Sie deren Bedeutung nach.

3. Unterstreichen Sie die kleinen Wörter (Adjektive und Adverbien, Zeitangaben, usw.) und schlagen Sie auch diese Wörter nach.

4. Gehen Sie den Text noch einmal durch und unterstreichen oder markieren Sie die Sätze, die besonders lang oder kompliziert sind, und auf die Sie folglich besonders achten müssen.

5. Übersetzen Sie den Text nun Satz für Satz.

6. Überprüfen Sie Ihren Text mit dem Originaltext und stellen Sie sicher, dass Sie nichts vergessen haben.

7. Lesen Sie Ihren Text noch einmal hinsichtlich korrekter Rechtschreibung, Zeichensetzung, Grammatik, Wortwahl und Satzbau durch.

Schritt für Schritt zur Mediation

1. Lesen Sie den Text mehrmals aufmerksam durch.

2. Schlagen Sie nur die Wörter nach, ohne die Sie den Text als Ganzes nicht verstehen würden. Verwenden Sie nicht zu viel Zeit, um jedes unbekannte Wort nachzuschlagen. Diese Zeit fehlt Ihnen später.

3. Notieren Sie die Antworten auf folgende Wh-Fragen: *Who ...?, When ...?, Where ...?, Why?*

    Achtung: Auf nicht alle Wh-Fragen gibt es eine Antwort, aber so finden Sie ganz schnell heraus, was die wichtigsten Punkte des Textes sind.

4. Gehen Sie den Text Absatz für Absatz durch und entscheiden Sie, welche Stellen Sie für Ihre Mediation benötigen. Markieren Sie diese Textstellen entsprechend.

5. Fassen Sie nun diese Textstellen auf Englisch zusammen.

6. Vergleichen Sie den Originaltext mit Ihrem Text. Haben Sie etwas vergessen? Steht in Ihrem Text etwas Falsches? Steht in Ihrem Text etwas Unwichtiges?

7. Lesen Sie Ihren Text hinsichtlich korrekter Rechtschreibung, Zeichensetzung, Grammatik, Wortwahl und Satzbau durch.

1 Aufgabentyp Übersetzung: Einen Text ins Deutsch übersetzen

Translate the text excerpt including the title freely into German. Remember to translate as closely as possible and as freely as necessary.

When it comes to integrating immigrants, friendship is the key

How do you integrate newcomers, and even long-standing residents who continue to live apart, into British society? [...]

First, it is a two-way process: both the host
5 society and the incomer have to adapt, though the latter has to do so more. Second, there is a balance to be struck between the fact that people of similar backgrounds want to cluster together and the belief that a good society
10 requires some mixing and sharing across social and ethnic lines. [...] Few British people say they do not want someone from another race as a neighbour and only about 30 per cent of people say they would prefer to live in an 15 area where everyone is from the same background. [...]

One appealing definition of an integrated society is one in which almost everyone is a potential friend. differences of race, class and 20 religion are not obstacles to personal trust, loyalty and even intimacy between individuals of very different backgrounds.

Source: David Goodhart, The Daily Telegraph,
24 January 2016; 167 words

Übung 1: Den Text verstehen

A   Lesen Sie den Text aufmerksam durch.

B   Die unten aufgelisteten Wörter sind Ihnen wahrscheinlich unbekannt. Schlagen Sie die deutsche Übersetzung der Wörter nach.

C   Fügen Sie weitere unbekannte Wörter hinzu und schlagen Sie auch diese nach.

English	German
long-standing	
host society	
to adapt	
though	
latter	
strike a balance	
to cluster together	
to require	
appealing	
obstacles	
trust	

Übung 2: Satz für Satz übersetzen

Nehmen Sie sich nun die Sätze einzeln vor und übersetzen Sie sie. Manche Sätze wurden schon für Sie begonnen. Sehen Sie sich die Lösungen erst an, nachdem Sie Übung 3 auf S. 52 gemacht haben.

1   When it comes to integrating immigrants, friendship is the key.

_____, *ist Freundschaft der Schlüssel.*

(Wichtig ist hier, „when it comes to" als Begriff zu behandeln.)

2   How do you integrate newcomers, and even long-standing residents who continue to live apart, into British society?

Wie integriert man _____ , *die immer noch*

für sich leben, in die britische Gesellschaft?

3 First, it is a two-way process: <u>both the host society and the incomer have to adapt, though the</u> <u>latter</u> has to do so more.

Zunächst handelt es sich um einen zweiseitigen Prozess: _____

_____ , _____ *sich*

_____ *mehr anstrengen muss.*

(Muss man „both" als „beide" übersetzen, oder gibt es bessere Formulierungen?)

4 Second, there is <u>a balance to be struck</u> between the fact that people of similar backgrounds want <u>to cluster together</u> and the belief that a good society <u>requires</u> some mixing and sharing <u>across social and ethnic lines.</u>

Zweitens muss _____, *und zwar zwischen der Tatsache, dass sich Menschen*

ähnlicher Herkunft gern _____, *und dem Glauben, dass sich eine gute*

Gesellschaft _____ *durchmischen und miteinander teilen*

_____ .

(„Requires" ist hier ein seltsames Verb. Welches deutsche Modalverb kann man verwenden, um dessen Sinn zu übertragen?)

5 <u>Few British people say</u> they do not want <u>someone from another race</u> as a neighbour and <u>only</u> <u>about 30 per cent of people</u> say they would prefer to live in an area <u>where everyone is from the</u> <u>same background.</u>

_____ *sagen, dass sie keinen Nachbarn* _____

haben wollen, und _____ *sagen, sie würden lieber in einer Gegend leben,*

_____ .

(Wie übersetzt man „British people"? Was ist hier mit „background" gemeint?)

6 <u>One appealing definition</u> of an integrated society is one in which <u>almost everyone is a potential</u> <u>friend</u>: differences of race, class and religion are <u>not obstacles</u> to personal <u>trust</u>, loyalty and <u>even</u> intimacy between individuals <u>of very different backgrounds.</u>

_____ *einer integrierten Gesellschaft ist die, in der* _____

_____ *: Unterschiede in Bezug auf Rasse, Klasse und Religion sind*

_____ *für persönliches* _____ *, Loyalität und*

_____ *Intimität zwischen Individuen* _____ .

(Achten Sie auf „not". Wie übersetzt man dies auf Deutsch?)

Übung 3: Eine Übersetzung beurteilen und überarbeiten

Sie sind nun vertraut mit dem Text. Sehen Sie sich bitte den unten stehenden Text an, der von einem anderen Schüler übersetzt wurde. Leider sind ein paar Dinge schiefgegangen: Wörter wurden falsch übersetzt, Grammatikfehler haben sich eingeschlichen und manche Passagen sind zu frei übertragen worden.

A   Suchen Sie die Fehler, unterstreichen Sie sie und schreiben Sie die Fehlerkategorie an den Rand.

B   Verwenden Sie Ihre Notizen aus den Übungen 1 und 2, um die Übersetzung zu verbessern. Der Text sollte stilistisch einwandfrei sein. Man darf nicht mehr erkennen, dass es sich eigentlich um eine Übersetzung handelt.

Wenn es dazu kommt, Einwanderer zu integrieren, ist Freundschaft der Schlüssel	Notizen
Wie integriert man Neukommer und sogar lange stehende Bewohner, die immer noch für sich leben, in die britische Gesellschaft? Zunächst ist es sich ein zweiseitiger Prozess: beide, die Gastgeber-Gesellschaft und die Hinzukommenden müssen sich anpassen, doch der zuletzt kommende muss das umso mehr tun. Zweitens gibt es ein Gleichgewicht, dass es einzuhalten gibt zwischen der Akzeptanz, dass Leute mit ähnlichem Hintergrund zusammenkleben wollen und dem Glauben, dass eine gute Gesellschaft mehr erforderte als ein bisschen Mixen und Teilen über soziale und ethnische Linien hinweg. Wenige Britische Menschen sagen, dass sie niemanden von einer anderen Rasse als Nachbarn haben wollen und nur ungefähr 30 Prozent dieser Menschen sagen, sie werden lieber in einer Gegend leben, wo jeder ist vom selben Hintergrund. Eine ansprechende Definition einer integrierten Gesellschaft ist eine, in der meistens jeder ein potenter Freund ist: Unterschiede zwischen Rasse, Klasse und Religion sind keine Hindernisse für persönliches Vertrauen, Loyalität und sogar Intimität zwischen Individuen verschiedenen Hintergrunds.	

2   Aufgabentyp Mediation: Einen Text auf Englisch zusammenfassen

Summarize the text in English in not more than 120 words.
One point will be deducted for every 10 words that you are over the word limit.

Lebensmittel: Zwischen Wertschätzung und Verschwendung

Jahr für Jahr landen in Deutschland 11 Millionen Tonnen Lebensmittel im Wert von circa 25 Milliarden Euro im Müll. [...]

Zur Verschwendung tragen alle bei: Hersteller, Landwirtschaft, Handel und Verbraucher.   5

Der verschwenderische Umgang mit Lebens-

mitteln wirkt sich negativ sowohl auf die Umwelt und die Ressourcen als auch die Versorgung vor allem der Bevölkerung in den ärmeren
10 Ländern aus.
Aus der Wertschätzung von Lebensmitteln ist inzwischen eher eine Geringschätzung geworden. Zurückzuführen ist dies auf den ständigen Preiskampf des Lebensmitteleinzelhan-
15 dels in Deutschland. In der Folge sind die Ausgaben für Nahrungs- und Genussmittel von 1950 mit 50 Prozent des Haushaltseinkommens auf aktuell nur noch 9,5 Prozent gesunken. Lebensmittel sind immer billiger gewor-
20 den. Und die "Geiz ist Geil"-Mentalität wird weiter geschürt, denn es vergeht kein Tag ohne Werbung mit neuen Sonderangeboten.

Der Trend zu Fast Food und Fertigprodukten hält ungebrochen an. Der veränderte Alltag
25 und die Zeitknappheit haben dazu geführt,

dass inzwischen fast 40 Prozent der Lebensmittelausgaben in der Außer-Haus-Verpflegung erfolgen – mit steigender Tendenz. [...]

Wer beim Einkauf und auch zu Hause einige Tipps beherzigt, kann dazu beitragen, dass we- 30 niger Nahrungsmittel verschwendet werden. [...]

Wir alle können jedoch schon heute damit beginnen, denn über die Hälfte aller Lebensmittelabfälle im Haushalt ist vermeidbar. Ein be- 35 wusster Umgang mit Lebensmitteln kann zu Einsparungen von 230 Euro pro Person und mehr führen. Damit tun Sie nicht nur Gutes für den Umwelt- und Klimaschutz, sondern schonen gleichzeitig Ihren Geldbeutel. 40

(Source: „Lebensmittel: Zwischen Wertschätzung und Verschwendung", website of the Verbraucherzentrale, 13 December 2016; 235 words)

Übung 1: Den Text lesen und verstehen

A   Lesen Sie den Text aufmerksam durch. Schlagen Sie eventuell unbekannte deutsche Wörter nach.

B   Teilen Sie den Text dann in Sinn- bzw. Handlungsabschnitte ein.

C   Vervollständigen Sie die Tabelle. Tragen Sie die Zeilennummern jedes Abschnitts ein. Schreiben Sie eine kurze Zusammenfassung des Abschnitts in Stichworten.

Zeilennummern	Zusammenfassung auf Deutsch
1–5	*So viel landet im Müll; die Beteiligten; die Auswirkungen*

Übung 2: Unwichtiges herausstreichen

Gehen Sie den Text nun noch einmal durch.

1   Streichen Sie unwichtige Passagen durch. (Die erste unwichtige Passage ist schon durchgestrichen.)

2   Unterstreichen Sie wichtige Wörter und Phrasen. (Die erste wichtige Passage ist schon hervorgehoben.)

Lebensmittel: Zwischen Wertschätzung und Verschwendung

Jahr für Jahr landen in Deutschland 11 Millionen Tonnen Lebensmittel im Wert von circa 25 Milliarden Euro im Müll. [...]

Zur Verschwendung tragen alle bei: Hersteller,
5 Landwirtschaft, Handel und Verbraucher.

Der verschwenderische Umgang mit Lebensmitteln wirkt sich negativ sowohl auf die Umwelt und die Ressourcen als auch die Versorgung vor allem der Bevölkerung in den ärmeren
10 Ländern aus.
Aus der Wertschätzung von Lebensmitteln ist inzwischen eher eine Geringschätzung geworden. Zurückzuführen ist dies auf den ständigen Preiskampf des Lebensmitteleinzelhan-
15 dels in Deutschland. In der Folge sind die Ausgaben für Nahrungs- und Genussmittel von 1950 mit 50 Prozent des Haushaltseinkommens auf aktuell nur noch 9,5 Prozent gesunken. Lebensmittel sind immer billiger geworden.
20 den. Und die "Geiz ist Geil"-Mentalität wird weiter geschürt, denn es vergeht kein Tag ohne Werbung mit neuen Sonderangeboten.

Der Trend zu Fast Food und Fertigprodukten hält ungebrochen an. Der veränderte Alltag und die Zeitknappheit haben dazu geführt, 25 dass inzwischen fast 40 Prozent der Lebensmittelausgaben in der Außer-Haus-Verpflegung erfolgen – mit steigender Tendenz. [...]

Wer beim Einkauf und auch zu Hause einige Tipps beherzigt, kann dazu beitragen, dass we- 30 niger Nahrungsmittel verschwendet werden. [...]

Wir alle können jedoch schon heute damit beginnen, denn über die Hälfte aller Lebensmittelabfälle im Haushalt ist vermeidbar. Ein be- 35 wusster Umgang mit Lebensmitteln kann zu Einsparungen von 230 Euro pro Person und mehr führen. Damit tun Sie nicht nur Gutes für den Umwelt- und Klimaschutz, sondern schonen gleichzeitig Ihren Geldbeutel. 40

(Source: „Lebensmittel: Zwischen Wertschätzung und Verschwendung“, website of the Verbraucherzentrale, 13 Dezember 2016; 235 words)

Übung 3: Beantworten von Wh-Fragen auf Englisch

Beantworten Sie nun die folgenden Wh-Fragen in einfachem Englisch. Formulieren Sie so einfach wie möglich.

1   How much food goes to waste every year?

_____

2   Who contributes to the huge amounts of waste?

_____

3   What are the consequences?

_____

4 How much money can you save if you are more responsible with food?

_____

5 **a** How do people value food?

_____

b What is the reason for this?

_____

6 How do people eat nowadays, and why?

_____

Übung 4: Einen fertigen Text schreiben

A Vergleichen Sie die Fragen, die Sie beantwortet haben, mit Ihren Markierungen im Text und überprüfen Sie, ob Sie etwas übersehen/vergessen haben.

B Wandeln Sie nun Ihre Antworten in einen Fließtext um.

_____

_____

_____

_____

_____

_____

_____

_____

_____

_____

_____

_____

TEIL D PRODUKTION

In diesem Aufgabenteil müssen Sie einen Aufsatz schreiben. Folgende Aufgbabentypen können in der Prüfung vorkommen:

- Das Verfassen eines Kommentars zu einem Thema.
- Das Schreiben einer Diskussion (auch „Vergleich" genannt).
- Die Beschreibung und Interpretation eines Bildes/Cartoons/Diagramms.

Es wird von Ihnen erwartet, dass Sie zwischen 270 und 330 Wörtern schreiben. Achten Sie unbedingt darauf, dieses Wörterlimit einzuhalten, denn sonst bekommen Sie Punktabzug!

Für diesen Aufgabenteil bekommen Sie maximal 40 BE. Sie sollten also intensiv an der Aufgabe arbeiten und sich ausreichend dafür Zeit nehmen (etwa 60 Minuten).

Wie gliedere ich den Schreibprozess?

Besonders wichtig ist die Phase der **Planung**. Hier sollten Sie sehr sorgfältig und intensiv arbeiten. Zum Planen gehören folgende Aspekte:

- Die Aufgabenstellung genau lesen und verstehen.
- Zum Thema brainstormen.
- Argumente/Punkte strukturieren und daraus eine Gliederung erstellen.
- Geeignete Beispiele finden.
- Ideen für eine angemessene Einleitung und einen passenden Schluss finden.
- Unpassendes verwerfen.

Im Anschluss an das Planen kommt das **Schreiben**. Wenn Sie im Vorfeld gute Arbeit geleistet haben, wird Ihnen dieser Teil leicht von der Hand gehen. Beachten Sie beim Schreiben, dass Sie nur auf ca. 40 Wörter für die Einleitung, ca. 40 Wörter für den Schluss und nicht mehr als 250 Wörter für den Hauptteil kommen sollten.

Die letzte Phase des Schreibprozesses ist die **Überarbeitung**. Sie ist nicht weniger wichtig als die anderen Phasen. Folgende Aspekte gehören zu dieser Phase:

- Den Text auf seine logische Struktur hin überprüfen.
- Besonderes Augenmerk auf Rechtschreibung, Zeichensetzung und Grammatik legen.
- Flüchtigkeitsfehler vermeiden.
- Auf Vollständigkeit hin überprüfen.

1 Das Verfassen eines Kommentars zu einem Thema

Bei diesem Aufgabentyp wägen Sie nicht Pro und Kontra einer Fragestellung gegeneinander ab, sondern Sie werden aufgefordert, Gründe für eine bestimmte Sachlage zusammenzustellen und möglicherweise auch Lösungsmöglichkeiten zu entwickeln, einen Sachverhalt zu beschreiben und mögliche Konsequenzen daraus aufzuzeigen.

Übung 1: Die Aufgabenstellung verstehen

Name the reasons why some young Muslims become radicalized and describe possible ways to prevent them from becoming radicalized.

A Schreiben Sie die Schlüsselwörter bezogen auf die Fragestellung auf.

_____

B Schreiben Sie die Operatoren bezogen auf die Art der Aufgabenstellung auf.

_____

C Schlagen Sie im Operatorenkatalog (S. 72) nach, was die Operatoren bedeuten.

_____

_____

Übung 2: Ideen sammeln

A Vervollständigen Sie die beiden angefangenen Ideensterne und notieren Sie alle Ihre Ideen.

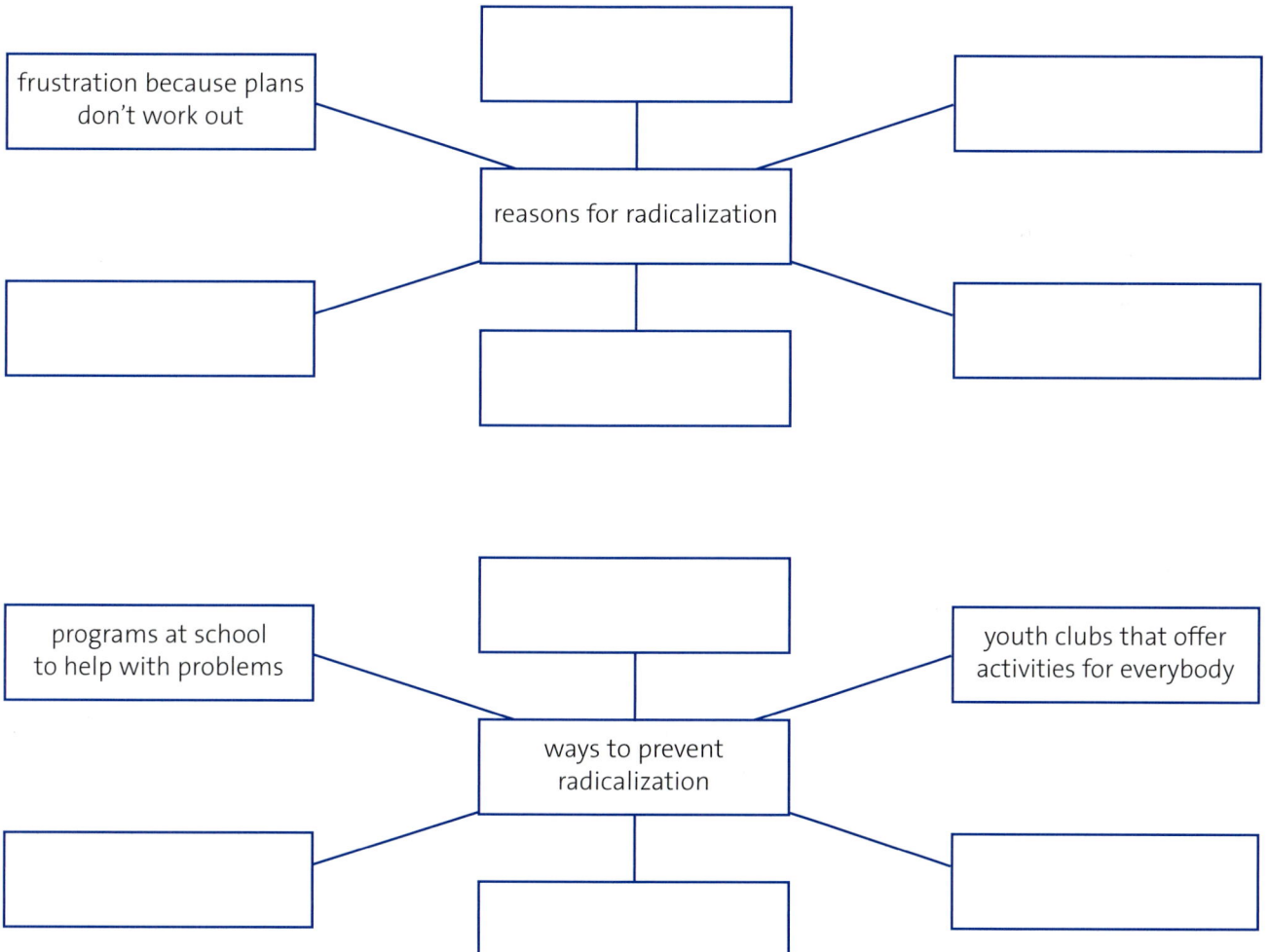

B Sehen Sie sich Ihre Ideen noch einmal genau an und verwerfen Sie jene, die Ihnen nicht gefallen, die nicht stichhaltig sind oder nicht zum Thema passen.

C Schreiben Sie passende Beispiele zu den Punkten, die Sie gesammelt haben.

D Nummerieren Sie Ihre Punkte und erstellen Sie somit eine Gliederung.

Übung 3: Eine Gliederung erstellen

Formen Sie Ihre Mindmap in eine Gliederung um, indem Sie deren Inhalte in eine Tabelle übertragen.

the reasons for a possible radicalization of young Muslims	
reason	example
frustration because plans don't work out	*they want to start a job/training and don't get invited to a job interview because of a foreign name or foreign looks*

ways to prevent radicalization	
idea	example
programs at school to help with problems	*help with homework, job application training, mentoring etc.*

Übung 4: Den Text schreiben

Um einen Text gut strukturiert zu schreiben, gibt es kleine Wörtchen – *connecting words* genannt – mit denen Sie in einen Absatz einleiten oder von einem Absatz zum anderen überleiten können.

A   Sortieren Sie diese *connecting words* in die Tabelle unten ein.

connecting words	
although ...	In addition, ...
apart from ...	In conclusion, ...
Another point to consider is this:	In my opinion, ...
As a consequence, ...	In spite of this, ...
As a result, ...	It makes sense to start by asking whether ...
Because of this, ...	Moreover, ...
even though ...	On the other hand, ...
except for ...	On the whole, ...
Finally, ...	Secondly, ...
Firstly, ... / First of all ...	That is why ...
For this reason ...	The issue I want to discuss here is ...
Furthermore, ...	Therefore, ...
However, ...	To sum up, ...
I am of the opinion that ...	We can clearly see that ...

das Thema einleiten	die eigene Meinung darlegen	Punkte/Argumente auflisten
eine These untermauern	**Ausnahmen einräumen**	**ein Gegenargument anführen**
einen Standpunkt begründen	**Auswirkungen oder Resultate beschreiben**	**die Argumentation zusammen-fassen und ein Fazit ziehen**

Achtung: Für diese Aufsatzform benötigen Sie nicht alle der oben aufgeführten strukturierenden Elemente/Formulierungshilfen. Für die Aufgabenstellung „Diskussion" jedoch schon, da hier die Pro- und Kontra-Seite diskutiert wird.

B Bringen Sie nun die Punkte Ihrer Gliederung in einen Fließtext. Achten Sie darauf, dass Sie strukturierende *connecting words* verwenden.

There are many reasons why radicalization takes place. _____

_____

_____

_____

_____

_____

How to prevent radicalization is a difficult subject. _____

_____

_____

_____

_____

Übung 5: Eine Einleitung und einen Schluss formulieren

A Lesen Sie sich die folgende Einleitung durch und beurteilen Sie sie. Schreiben Sie eine bessere Version, wenn Sie Handlungsbedarf sehen.

Recently, a terrorist attack in Manchester by a young Muslim shocked the world. I am wondering why young men get radicalized and what can be done against it.

Beurteilung: _____

_____

Bessere Version: _____

_____

_____

_____

B Lesen Sie sich den folgenden Schluss durch und beurteilen Sie ihn. Schreiben Sie eine bessere Version, wenn Sie Handlungsbedarf sehen.

In conclusion, I would like to say that not enough has been done to integrate young Muslims. At the moment, many feel that they cannot find success, and that they have no future, and that they are caught between two cultures. In order to show them how they can find a place in society, we need to offer them more help, like more courses, more support, more activities. So to sum up, I want to say that more effort needs to be made to make young Muslims proud to be Muslim and proud to be part of our society.

Beurteilung: _____

_____

Bessere Version: _____

_____

_____

2 Das Schreiben einer Diskussion

Bei diesem Aufgabentyp geht es um das Ausloten eines Themas. Sie werden aufgefordert, das Pro und das Kontra einer Fragestellung gegeneinander abzuwägen.

Übung 1: Die Aufgabenstellung verstehen

"In economic terms, only the West benefits from globalization." Discuss this statement talking about the pros and cons of a globalized world.

A   Schreiben Sie die Schlüsselwörter bezogen auf den Inhalt der Frage auf.

_____

B   Schreiben Sie die Operatoren bezogen auf die Art der Aufgabenstellung auf.

_____

C   Schlagen Sie im Operatorenkatalog (S. 72) nach, was die Operatoren bedeuten.

_____

Übung 2: Argumente sammeln und ordnen

A   Suchen Sie je drei Pro- und Kontra-Argumente und tragen Sie diese in die Tabelle ein.
B   Entscheiden Sie sich, welchen Standpunkt Sie vertreten. Machen Sie ein Kreuz an der entsprechenden Stelle.
C   Bringen Sie Ihre Argumente in eine Reihenfolge.
   A   Die Seite, die Sie nicht vertreten: Nummerieren Sie vom stärksten zum schwächsten Argument.
   B   Die Seite, die Sie vertreten: Nummerieren Sie vom schwächsten zum stärksten Argument.

"In economic terms, only the West benefits from globalization."			
a globalized world is good		a globalized world is bad	
My opinion: a globalized world is good ☐		My opinion: a globalized world is bad ☐	
1		1	
2		2	
3		3	

Übung 3: Beispiele finden

Übertragen Sie Ihre Argumente in untenstehendes Schema und finden Sie passende Beispiele.

Argument 1: _____

Example: _____

Argument 2: _____

Example: _____

Argument 3: _____

Example: _____

Gegenargument 1: _____

Example: _____

Gegenargument 2: _____

Example: _____

Gegenargument 3: _____

Example: _____

Übung 4: Eine fertige Diskussion sortieren

A   Bei dem untenstehenden Teil einer Diskussion ist einiges schiefgegangen. Bringen Sie die einzelnen Absätze in die richtige Reihenfolge.

	Additionally, I would like to mention that outsourcing can be a job generator in many countries. If a company didn't go to another country for production, for example, there wouldn't be any new jobs there.

	I would like to start with the fact that we all benefit from cheaper prices – and not just people in the West. Due to a global market there is a wider selection of products to choose from. This competition is good for the customer who can look for the best price of a product.

	Furthermore, many people in the West don't have a job anymore because a company moved to another country.

	On the other hand, many companies exploit the workers in developing countries. They pay them very low wages and therefore they can keep production costs low, which makes the price of a product cheaper.

B   Beurteilen Sie die Qualität des Textauszuges. Notieren Sie Ihre Einschätzung in Stichworten.

1 _____

_____

2 _____

_____

3 _____

_____

4 _____

_____

C   Schreiben Sie die Diskussion auf Basis der Argumente in 4 A.

_____

_____

_____

_____

_____

_____

_____

_____

_____

Übung 5: Eine gute Einleitung schreiben

Vermutlich haben Sie erkannt, dass die Einleitung und der Schluss noch fehlen. Darum wollen wir uns jetzt kümmern.

A   Sammeln Sie Ideen für eine Einleitung.

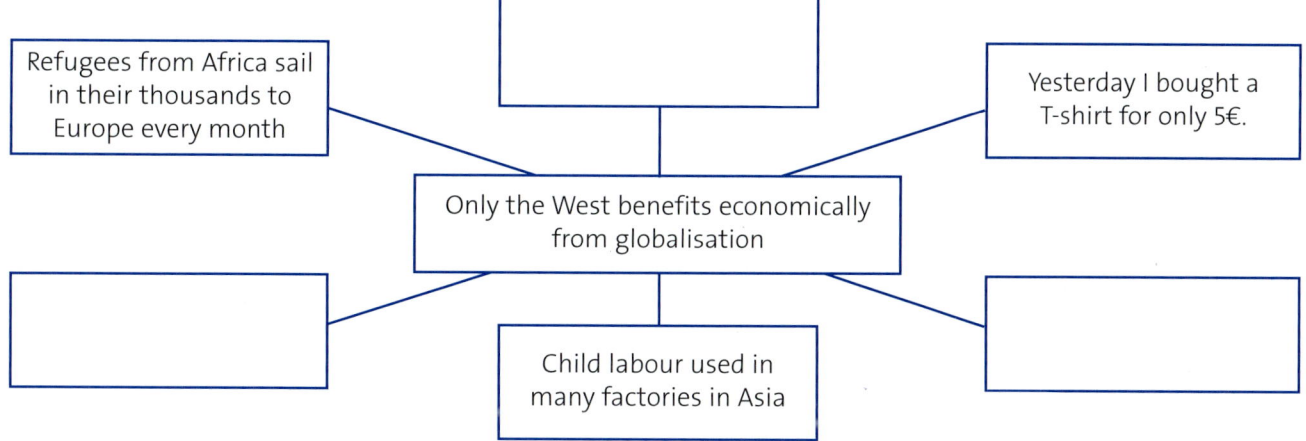

Refugees from Africa sail in their thousands to Europe every month

Yesterday I bought a T-shirt for only 5€.

Only the West benefits economically from globalisation

Child labour used in many factories in Asia

> **Tipps:**
> - Besonders gut eignen sich für die Einleitung aktuelle Ereignisse, Nachrichtenmeldungen, Statistiken oder eigene Erlebnisse.
> - Beenden Sie die Einleitung mit der Fragestellung.

B Verfassen Sie die Einleitung.

_____

_____

_____

Übung 6: Einen passenden Schluss schreiben

> **Tipp:**
> - Im Schlussteil einer Diskussion ziehen Sie ein Fazit dessen, was Sie geschrieben haben. Dafür können Sie ein Argument wiederholen, das Sie besonders wichtig fanden. Oder Sie schreiben hier explizit Ihre Meinung – bisher haben Sie sich ja um ein neutrales Abwägen des Für und Wider bemüht. Sie können auch Ihre Leser zu etwas appellieren, also zu einem bestimmten Verhalten aufrufen.

A Beurteilen Sie den abgedruckten Schluss. Ziehen Sie für Ihre Beurteilung den Tippkasten oben zurate.

To conclude, I would like to stress again the fact that many companies exploit workers in third-world countries. They pay them low wages and they make them work in inhumane conditions. Therefore, people out there, buy local and don't be stingy!

B Optimieren Sie den Schluss, falls nötig.

_____

_____

_____

3 Die Beschreibung und Interpretation eines Bildes/Cartoons/ Diagramms

Bei diesem Aufgabentyp kann das Material ein Cartoon, Foto oder Schaubild sein. Gehen Sie nach dem folgenden Drei-Schritte-Schema vor:

1. Beschreiben Sie zunächst das Material. Was ist auf dem Cartoon, dem Foto oder dem Schaubild zu sehen?

2. Interpretieren Sie die zentrale Aussage des Materials. Was bedeutet der Cartoon, das Foto oder das Diagramm? Welche Botschaft will das Material vermitteln?

3. Nehmen Sie selbst Stellung zur Darstellung / zum Inhalt. Handelt es sich um ein relevantes Problem? Sind Sie derselben Meinung? Sind Sie anderer Meinung?

Auch hier sollten Sie wieder planen, bevor Sie schreiben und überarbeiten.

Übung 1: Die Aufgabenstellung verstehen

Describe the cartoon and interpret the message of the cartoon concerning overconsumption and the consequences for humanity.

(Source: cartoonstock/Chris Madden)

A Schreiben Sie die Schlüsselwörter bezogen auf den Inhalt der Frage auf.

_____

B Schreiben Sie die Operatoren bezogen auf die Art der Aufgabenstellung auf.

_____

C Schlagen Sie im Operatorenkatalog (S. 72) nach, was die Operatoren bedeuten.

_____

_____

Übung 2: Beschreibung des Cartoons: Notizen machen

Betrachten Sie den abgedruckten Cartoon genau. Machen Sie sich Notizen.

Tipp:
- Schreiben Sie Ihre Notizen direkt neben den Cartoon. Arbeiten Sie mit Pfeilen. So sehen Sie ganz genau, ob Sie bereits alles abgedeckt haben, was die Beschreibung des Cartoons ausmacht.

Übung 3: Welche Informationen stimmen?

Lesen Sie sich die folgenden Aussagen zum Cartoon durch und kreuzen Sie jene an, die richtig sind.

1 ☐ The car is driving down a hill.

2 ☐ In the car there are two people.

3 ☐ The road turns from smooth to rough.

4 ☐ The man is driving an SUV.

5 ☐ The car is driving on a symbolic road.

6 ☐ The car stands for something else.

7 ☐ The woman who is sitting in the front seat is worrying about the future.

8 ☐ The man who is driving the car is trying to calm his wife down.

9 ☐ The man is happy about his car because with it they don't notice the bumpy road.

Übung 4: Die zentrale Aussage des Cartoons bestimmen

A Was „bedeutet" der Cartoon? Kreuzen Sie die richtige Aussage an.

1 ☐ People consume too much.

2 ☐ People have a bad conscience about destroying the environment.

3 ☐ We are destroying our earth but instead of stopping the madness we invent more and more things for our convenience.

4 ☐ Overconsumption destroys the earth.

5 ☐ People try to ignore the damage they do to the environment.

6 ☐ The roads are in a devastating state and something has to be done about it.

B Möglicherweise haben Sie gezögert, welche Aussage die richtige ist, weil in den meisten Aussagen ein wahrer Kern ist. Kommentieren Sie die Aussagen, die Sie auch in die engere Auswahl gezogen haben, gegen die Sie sich aber letzten Endes doch entschieden haben.

1 _____

_____

2 _____

_____

3 _____

_____

4 _____

_____

5 _____

_____

6 _____

_____

Übung 5: Die Beschreibung und die Interpretation verfassen

Schreiben Sie nun Ihren Text. Sie können die angekreuzten Aussagen von Übung 3 und 4 verwenden. Orientieren Sie sich an der Strukturierungshilfe neben den Schreibzeilen. Der Hauptteil des Texts soll auf der Beschreibung und der Interpretation liegen.

Auch für diese Aufgabe gibt es nützliche Formulierungshilfen, die Ihren Text strukturieren und präziser machen. Wählen Sie für Ihren Text die geeigneten Ausdrücke aus der Liste auf der nächsten Seite aus.

introduction _____

_____

description _____

_____

_____

_____

analysis _____

_____

_____

_____

your opinion _____

_____

_____

Tipp:

- Wenn Sie den Cartoon / die Anzeige / das Foto beschreiben, sollten Sie immer das *present progressive* für das verwenden, was Sie sehen.

Nützliche Ausdrücke für die Bildanalyse

Thematik
This is a cartoon about …

Bildelemente
In the foreground/background/middle we can see …
At the top/bottom / In the middle there is …
The caption/label/speech bubble/thought bubble tells us that …

Interpretation
It looks as if the man is about to …
The woman has probably just …-ed
The person on the left/right seems to have a … expression.
He/She seems to be …-ing

Aussage und Absichten
The picture is intended to amuse/puzzle/shock/surprise the viewer.
The artist wants to inform the viewer about …
The advertisement is trying to persuade us to …
The cartoon is satirizing/making fun of …
The advertisement is promoting …
The advertisement is campaigning against …
The image warns us against the dangers of …
The message of the advertisement/cartoon is clear: …
The message of the cartoon/advertisement is ambiguous/obscure/unclear.
Are we to think that … or …?

Eigene Meinung und Stellungnahme
Personally, I find the picture quite/very amusing/clever/confusing/disturbing.
In my view, the advertisement/cartoon conveys/fails to convey its message effectively.
At first I thought the picture was …
However, on closer viewing it is clear that the picture is …

Themen, die mit dem Bild verbunden sind
This brings us to the wider subject of …
This leads us on to the subject of …
The picture invites us to consider …

THEMENWORTSCHATZ

Globalisation	Globalisierung	Globalisation	Globalisierung
to affect	sich auswirken auf	import tax	Einfuhrzoll
agriculture	Landwirtschaft	importer	Importeur
Americanization	Amerikanisierung	infrastructure	Infrastruktur
availability	Verfügbarkeit	to invest in	investieren in
to benefit from	profitieren von	to lead to	führen zu
carbon emission	Kohlenstoffausstoß	local	lokal
carbon footprint	CO_2-Bilanz	low wages	niedrige Löhne
child labour	Kinderarbeit	to manufacture	hersteller, produzieren
competition	Wettbewerb	manufacturer	Hersteller
company	Firma, Unternehmer	multinational	multinationaler Konzern
conditions	Bedingungen	negotiate	aushandeln
to consume	verbrauchen, konsumieren	opportunity	Möglichkeit
consumer	Verbraucher/in	produce (n)	Erzeugnis(se)
consumer goods	Konsumgüter	produce	herstellen
consumer society	Konsumgesellschaft	producer	Hersteller
consumption	Verbrauch	to protect	schützen
corporation	Unternehmer, Konzern	quality	Qualität
to damage	schaden	to redistribute	umverteilen
dependent on	abhängig von	restriction	Beschränkung
developed country	Industrieland	to result in	führen zu
developing country	Entwicklungsland	retail	Einzelhandels-
development	Entwicklung	retailer	Einzelhändler
earn	verdienen	security	Sicherheit
economic	wirtschaftlich	social	gesellschaftlich
employment	Beschäftigung	society	Gesellschaft
employ	beschäftigen	sustainability	Nachhaltigkeit
environment	Umwelt	sustainable	zukunftsfähig
to exploit	ausbeuten	sweat shop	Sweatshop
exporter	Exporteur	telecommunications	Telekommunikation
factory	Fabrik, Betrieb	trade	Handel
free trade	Freihandel	to trade (with)	handeln mit
global	global, international	unemployed	Arbeitslose
goods	Waren, Produkte	unemployment	Arbeitslosigkeit
growth	Wachstum	variety	Auswahl
to have an impact on	eine Auswirkung auf haben	wealth	Reichtum
impact	Auswirkung	wholesale	Großhandels-
import tax	Einfuhrzoll	to work in hazardous conditions	unter gefährlichen Bedingungen arbeiten

migration	Migration/Einwanderung	migration	Migration/Einwanderung
to assimilate	assimilieren	inequality	Ungleichheit
to be prejudiced against	Vorurteile haben gegen(über)	to integrate into	integrieren in
assimilation	Assimilation	integration	Integration
catastrophe	Katastrophe	menial work	untergeordnete Arbeit
civil war	Bürgerkrieg	migrant	Migrant/in, Einwanderer/in
community	Gemeinde	to migrate	migrieren, einwandern
cultural diversity	kulturelle Vielfalt	minority	Minderheit
custom	Brauch	multicultural	multikulturell
to discriminate against	jdn. diskriminieren	multiculturalism	Multikulturalismus
discrimination	Diskriminierung	newcomer	Ankömmling
to displace	verdrängen, vertreiben	persecution	Verfolgung
diversity	Vielfalt	population	Bevölkerung
to enrich	bereichern	poverty	Armut
equal	gleich (berechtigt)	prejudice	Vorurteil
equality	Gleichheit	racial	Rassen-
ethnic origin	ethnische Herkunft	racism	Rassismus
to experience	erfahren, erleben.	racist	(ad) rassistisch, (n) racist
extremist	Extremist/in	radicalise	radikalisieren
fair/fairly	gerecht	refugee camp	Flüchtlingslager
famine-stricken	von Hunger bedroht	resentment	Unmut, Groll, Ressentiment
fundamentalist	Fundamentalist/in	right	Recht
to grow up	aufwachsen	to seek refuge	Zuflucht suchen
heritage	Herkunft, Erbe	shelter	Unterkunft
human trafficker	Schleuser/in, Menschenhändler/in	tolerance	Toleranz
to identify with	sich identifizieren mit	to treat	behandeln
identity	Identität	war	Krieg
immigrant	Einwanderer/in	workforce	Erwerbstätige, Erwerbsbevölkerung
immigration	Einwanderung	xenophobia	Fremdenfeindlichkeit, Ausländerhass

environment	Umwelt
to adapt to	sich anpassen an
acid rain	saurer Regen
to be in sb's best interests	in jds Interesse sein
to become extinct	aussterben
biodiversity	Artenvielfalt
carbon dioxide	Kohlendioxid
carbon footprint	CO_2-Bilanz
to cause	verursachen
climate change	Klimawandel
coal	Kohle
consumption	Verbrauch
to contaminate	etw verunreinigen
crop	(Anbau-)Pflanzen
to damage	schädigen
deforestation	Abholzung
to deplete	erschöpfen
disaster	Katastrophe
drought	Dürre
drought-stricken	von Dürre betroffen
ecological	ökologisch
ecology	Ökologie
ecosystem	Ökosystem
emission	Ausstoß
to emit	ausstoßen, ausstrahlen
environment	Umwelt
environmental	Umwelt-
environmental impact	Umweltbelastung
environmental protection	Umweltschutz
far-reaching consequences	weitreichende Folgen
flood	Überschwemmung
fossil fuel	fossiler Brennstoff
fuel	Brennstoff
to generate	erzeugen
glacier	Gletscher
global warming	globale Erwärmung, Erderwärmung

environment	Umwelt
greenhouse gas	Treibhausgas
habitat	Lebensraum
human-induced	durch Menschen verursacht
ice cap	Polkappe
mass extinction	Massenausrottung
measure	Maßnahme
melt	schmelzen
natural	natürlich
natural resources	Rohstoffe
non-renewable	nicht erneuerbar
overpopulation	Überbevölkerung
ozone layer	Ozonschicht
pesticide	Schädlingsbekämpfungsmittel
to pollute	verschmutzen
pollution	Umweltverschmutzung
power station	Kraftwerk
to preserve	konservieren, schonen
to produce energy	Energie erzeugen
to protect	schützen
raw material	Rohstoff(e)
to recycle	recyceln, wiederverwerten
to reduce	reduzieren
to release	freisetzen
resource	Ressource
responsibility	Verantwortung
responsible	verantwortlich
to save the environment	die Umwelt retten
sea level	Meeresspiegel
solar panel	Sonnenkollektor
solution	Lösung
species	Art(en)
to survive	überleben
toxic	giftig
to use up	aufbrauchen
to warm	erwärmen
waste	Müll

OPERATOREN

Die Prüfungsaufgaben werden mit so genannten Operatoren (Schlüsselwörtern) formuliert, damit es klar ist, wie Sie die Aufgabe herangehen. Bei der Formulierung der Arbeitsanweisungen von Prüfungsaufgaben werden in der Regel nur die hier unten aufgelisteten Operatoren benutzt.

Operator(en)	Übersetzung	Definition
comment on	Stellung nehmen	zu einem Sachverhalt oder einer Aussage unter Verwendung von Fachwissen eine begründete eigene Meinung darstellen.
compare	vergleichen/ gegenüberstellen	Ähnlichkeiten und Unterschiede ermitteln und aufzeigen
complete	vervollständigen/ ausfüllen	relevante/erfragte Informationen/Aspekte in Stichpunkten aufzählen.
contrast	vergleichen/	Ähnlichkeiten und Unterschiede ermitteln und aufzeigen
depict	darstellen	Sachverhalte o. Ä. und deren Bezüge sowie Zusammenhänge aufzeigen
describe	beschreiben	Aussagen oder Sachverhalte in eigenen Worten strukturiert verdeutlichen
discuss	erörtern	eine These oder Problemstellung unter Abwägen von Pro- und Kontraargumenten hinterfragen und zu einem eigenen Urteil gelangen
explain	erklären	beschreiben oder im Detail definieren/erläutern
fill in	ausfüllen/ vervollständigen	relevante/erfragte Informationen/Aspekte in Stichpunkten aufzählen.
interpret	interpretieren	auf der Grundlage einer Analyse Sinnzusammenhänge aus Materialien methodisch reflektiert erschließen, um zu einer schlüssigen Gesamtauslegung zu gelangen
list	aufzählen/nennen	Aspekte/Fakten aus dem Gehörten oder Gelesenen auflisten/nennen. (keine ausformulierten Sätze!)
match	Zusammengehöriges finden	Aussagen zu „Ausdrücken" oder Bildern zuordnen. Teile, die zusammengehören, verknüpfen oder verbinden.
name	nennen/aufzählen	Aspekte/Fakten aus dem Gehörten oder Gelesenen auflisten/nennen. (keine ausformulierten Sätze!)
point out	darstellen	Sachverhalte o. Ä. und deren Bezüge sowie Zusammenhänge aufzeigen
put into the context of	einordnen	Texte oder Sachverhalte unter Verwendung von Vorwissen begründet in einen genannten Zusammenhang stellen
relate	in Beziehung setzen	einen Aspekt oder (Teil-)Aspekte des Ausgangstextes mit anderem Material begründet in Beziehung setzen
summarize/ sum up	zusammenfassen	(ausgehend von einem Einleitungssatz) die wesentlichen Aussagen eines Textes in strukturierter und komprimierter Form in ei-genen Worten wiedergeben.
tick	ankreuzen	eine richtige Aussage/Antwort, eine Zeichnung oder ein Bild ankreuzen.
translate freely	frei von einer Sprache in die andere übertragen	übertrage den Text frei vom Englischen ins Deutsche/vom Deutschen ins Englische, inhaltlich sollte der Text nicht reduziert werden. (Sprachliche Strukturen sind frei wählbar.)

Abschlussprüfung

Englisch

Lösungsheft

Fachoberschule
Hessen

Musterprüfung 1

1 Hörverstehen

event on November 28th	For 24 hours people will live without shopping.
participants	anyone
necessity of the event	People should think about what they buy and who they buy it from and what effect their purchases have on the environment and developing countries.
achievements during the event	You will get your life back because constant shopping consumes a lot of free time that will be available again.
current important topics	the environment and poverty
reasons for the topics being important	20% of the world population are consuming 80% of the earth's natural resources. We are destroying the earth and making people poor.
consequences of the event	It makes you think about your behaviour and what impacts it has.

Transkript des Hörtextes

Reporter: Today for the most of America, it is Black Friday, the day after Thanksgiving when nearly everybody goes shopping at the sales! It's the busiest shopping day of the year. However, for some it's Buy Nothing Day. With me is Sheila Smith, the organiser of Buy Nothing Day in Chicago. Sheila, what is Buy Nothing Day?

Sheila: Buy Nothing Day is quite simple. For 24 hours you live without shopping! Buy Nothing Day is a simple idea, which challenges our consumer society by asking us not to shop for a whole day. Anyone can take part provided they spend a day without spending!

Reporter: Why do you think Buy Nothing Day is necessary?

Sheila: As consumers, we should question the products we buy and the companies who produce them. The idea is to make people stop and think about what and how much they buy. These choices affect the environment and developing countries.

Reporter: But don't people enjoy shopping?

Sheila: Society has programmed us to spend, even when we don't need to. We need to change our behavior.

Reporter: Who is in charge of Buy Nothing Day?

Sheila: Nobody and everybody. It's your day, so get involved! Tell all your friends and refuse to shop today.

Reporter: So people just stay home and that's it?

Sheila: No, we also have events. There's a clothes exchange, where you exchange clothes with others instead of buying new ones. There's are sit-ins in front of various department stores. And there's are zombie walks around malls; all the zombies wear a sign saying "I'm a consumer".

Reporter: But what does it achieve?

Sheila: It's tough to last 24 hours without spending any money, but you'll realise how much it uses up your free time. For 24 hours you get your life back and that's a big achievement! We want people to make a commitment to consuming less, recycling more and challenging companies to clean up their environmental practices.

Reporter: Is shopping that bad?

Sheila: Shopping itself isn't bad. It's what we buy and how we buy that are bad. Our consumption leads to bad working conditions in developing countries and environmental damage.

Reporter: Is one day really going to make a difference?

Sheila: Buy Nothing Day isn't about just one day – it's a lasting change to your lifestyle. We aim to make Buy Nothing Day stick in your mind so you think about what you buy and the impact it has on the environment.

2 Leseverstehen

Wofür stehen Luftballons normalerweise?	für das Feiern
Was haben Kinder in Bangladesh mit Lufballons zu tun?	Sie arbeiten in den Luftballonfabriken, sortieren sie der Farbe nach und tragen zu schwere Lasten.
Wann beginnt und endet ihr Arbeitstag?	Er beginnt um 6 Uhr morgens und endet um 17 Uhr abends.
Warum arbeiten so viele Kinder für so wenig Geld?	Die Familien sind sehr arm und die Kinder müssen mitverdienen. Manche Mütter sind alleinerziehend, manche Väter arbeiten, aber ihr Verdienst reicht doch nicht.
Wie viele Kinder arbeiten in Bangladesch?	Im Alter von 10 bis 14 Jahren sind es eine Million Kinder, im Alter von 5 bis 14 Jahren sind es beinahe fünf Millionen.
Wo arbeiten die Kinder?	in Fabriken, Werkstätten, Haushalten, Bahnhöfen, Märkten
Unter welchen Arbeitsbedingungen arbeiten viele Kinder?	Die Arbeit ist oft gefährlich und viele bekommen geringen oder gar keinen Lohn.
Welche Konsequenzen hat die Arbeit für die Kinder?	Sie erfahren keine Bildung und bleiben immer arm.

3 Mediation

3.1

Warum Sie Ihre umweltfreundliche Baumwolltragtasche 131 Mal benutzen müssen, um grün zu sein

Baumwolltaschen, die viele Supermärkte anbieten, sind vielleicht weniger „grün" als Plastiktüten – und verstärken möglicherweise die globale Erwärmung, sagen Wissenschaftler. Da eine größere Menge an Energie für die Herstellung einer Stofftasche gebraucht wird als für eine aus Plastik, muss eine Baumwolltasche 131 Mal benutzt werden, um dieselbe Auswirkung auf die Umwelt zu haben wie ihr Gegenstück aus Plastik. Die meisten von uns nutzen diese Taschen jedoch nur 51 Mal, bevor sie weggeworfen werden, wie Wissenschaftler herausfanden.

Papiertüten müssen drei Mal genutzt werden, um umwelttechnisch genauso effektiv zu sein wie dünne Plastiktüten, während Tüten aus festem Plastik vier Mal benutzt werden müssen, um die Umwelt weniger zu belasten.

Eine dünne Plastiktüte aus HDPE (Polyethylen mit hoher Dichte) zu benutzen entspricht der Erzeugung von 1,57 kg Kohlendioxid, dem Treibhausgas, das Wissenschaftlern zufolge zur globalen Erwärmung führt. Eine Baumwolltasche müsste 171 Mal wiederverwendet werden, um dieselbe Menge an CO_2 auszustoßen. Die normalerweise in China produzierten Baumwolltaschen haben eine größere Auswirkung auf die Umwelt, weil Wasser und Dünger für deren Produktion benötigt werden, sie transportiert werden müssen und mehr Gewicht aufweisen. Die „Daily Mail" ist mit ihrer „Verbannt die Tüten"-Kampagne federführend bei den Bemühungen, wo immer möglich Plastiktüten zu vermeiden, um die Umwelt zu schützen. Peter Woodall sagte stellvertretend für die Verpackungsvereinigung „Packaging and Films Association", die Plastiktütenproduzenten vertritt: „Reduzieren, wiederverwenden, recyceln – darum geht es letzten Endes."

3.2

There is something cheaper than cheap clothes

How would you like that – every week something new to wear for no money at all? Well, there are so-called clothes-exchange parties all over Germany. You go there with clothes to give away and you come back with new clothes. According to Greenpeace, we hardly wear many of the clothes we have, yet people are spending more and more money on clothes. Activists and NGOs are encouraging sustainable living and better standards in the textile industry. But although sustainable clothing is seen as untrendy, some designers have started to upcycle clothes. The market for alternative fashion is small but growing. You can exchange clothes, borrow clothes or make them yourself. And you can go to those clothes-exchange parties. (118 words)

4 Produktion

Some people are really creative when it comes to buying clothes. They go to second-hand stores or buy them at the flea market. The latest trend is to go to a party where people bring old clothes and exchange them with other people's old clothes. Is this crazy or is it the first step to be responsible when it comes to clothes?

Many people say that we consume too much. We buy too many clothes for too little money. When we don't like something anymore we throw it away, even though it might still be good. Because we don't want to pay a lot of money for what we buy we go to cheap chains. But the problem with those chains is that they have their cheap clothes produced in developing countries where they do not pay the workers a lot of money. Additionally, there is a lot of child labour in these countries, because the families are so poor that even the children have to work. If that wasn't enough also the working conditions are bad. It is hot in the factories, it is not safe in the factories and people have to work long hours. If we finally decided that we don't want to support this nightmare anymore, something might change. We should no longer buy from these companies but also not from designer companies who do the same thing, with only one difference: their clothes are more expensive in order to make the company owners rich. So why not wear clothes until they fall apart or exchange clothes with other people when we don't like them anymore, or bring them to second-hand shops or other places? (279 words)

MUSTERPRÜFUNG 2

1 Hörverstehen

recent development concerning prices	They have increased on average by 2.6 percent a year.
main things affecting the price of food	drought, currency changes, technological innovations, geo-political power games
importance of oil for food prices	Oil is used for transportation, as food is transported across the world; oil by-products are used to make fertiliser.
uses for corn	Main food staple across the world; also used to produce bio-fuel.
consequences of improved living standards in India and China	More people are eating meat, which requires a lot of grain.
two factors that would lead to cheaper food prices	change our consumption; reduce human population

Transkript des Hörtextes

Over the past two decades, food prices have risen 2.6 percent a year on average. In this news report we will examine what factors influence the price of food.

There are a multitude of geopolitical factors that can influence global supply chains overnight. Drought is one of the main problems facing food growers. For example, drought in Africa helped increase the global price of sugar in 2016, as much of the cane crop was lost. At the same time, Brazil, the largest producer of sugar in the world, saw its currency decrease in value against the US dollar, making sugar more expensive on the global market. These two factors made the price of sugar rise by 10% within a few months in the second half of 2016.

However, prices can also drop quickly due to short-term factors. For example, technological innovation can also play a part. The use of fracking in the USA led to a dramatic downturn in the price of oil in 2014. Normally oil-producing countries would have reduced oil production to make up for their losses. However, Saudi Arabia decided to continue oil production at a high rate despite the fall in price just in order to undermine Iranian oil revenues. The price of food – transported by fuel-guzzling ships – dropped as a consequence. This is a good example of how technological know-how and geo-political power games affected the oil market at the same time.

Labour costs can affect the price of food, but this is usually not very noticeable. More important are tariffs which countries can impose on each other's exports.

Other examples of factors that can affect the price of food are war, animal diseases.

But such factors, while they may affect the ups and downs in the short term, don't affect the long-term rise in world food prices. Factors that affect the long-term price of food are many. First of all, food is transported great distances across the world. Coffee, for example, comes from Brazil to Europe. Meat is exported from Australia to China. Another factor is our need to use limited resources. Ships use oil. Oil is a limited resource. While oil prices have dropped significantly in recent years, nevertheless its price will rise in the near future, as oil reserves grow smaller. Oil prices also affect farming, as oil by-products are a large component of fertilizer, which is used to grow grain.

Corn, one of the main staples of the world's diet, is increasingly being produced as a bio-fuel. That takes a lot of corn out of the global food supply, again raising prices. The USA now uses 40 percent of its corn crop to make bio-fuels.

As countries like China and India get richer, more people around the world are adopting the Western diet, of which meat forms a large part. It takes more grain to feed the animals needed for meat than is needed to provide meals based on grain and vegetables. A higher demand for meat means higher grain prices.

Perhaps the single-most important factor affecting the price of food is the increasing number of mouths to feed.

There seems to be no end in sight to the dramatic annual increase in the world's population. As long as we have limited resources and an increasing population, we will see food prices continue to rise throughout the world.

There are only two ways in which prices might fall permanently. Firstly, if we radically change our consumption. Secondly, if we reduce the world population. But neither of these seem likely to happen soon.

2 Leseverstehen

2.1

The gadgets that are illegally transported to Africa are *broken TVs, computers, microwaves and refrigerators.*

2.2

This happens because *it is cheaper to transport them there than to recycle them in their countries of origin.*
In Africa the electronic gadgets are *sold to locals without being tested before. Then they are sold again.*

2.3

Other components of this electronic scrap are *gold, iron, copper, silver, aluminium and palladium but also toxic substances like mercury and cadmium.*

2.4

People come into contact with these substances because *they get into the water and into the air and they can also be found in vegetables and fruit.*
Britain ranks position number five concerning *throwing away things per person* and position number six *concerning the overall production of e-waste.*

2.6

The solution to e-waste is *to minimize consumption and increase recycling.*
The wealthiest nations of Europe *produce the largest amount of e-waste per head of population.*

3 Mediation

3.1

Liebe jenseits der Grenzen: gemischt ethnische Beziehungen nehmen in Großbritannien zu

Großbritannien wird zu einem ethnischen Schmelztiegel und verzeichnet, laut offizieller Zahlen, in den letzten zehn Jahren einen großen Anstieg in der Anzahl von Beziehungen und Ehen über ethnische Grenzen hinweg.

Aber während die Anzahl der Menschen mit schwarzem, asiatischem oder gemischtrassigem Hintergrund, die mit jemandem aus einer anderen ethnischen Gruppe einen Hausstand gründen, steigt, bleiben weiße Menschen mit großem Abstand die isolierteste Gruppe im privaten Bereich. Neue Auswertungen von Volkszählungsdaten zeigen, dass die Zahl der Menschen in England und Wales, die mit einer Person, die einer anderen Ethnie angehört, zusammenleben oder verheiratet sind, in den 10 Jahren seit der letzten Volkszählung sprunghaft angestiegen ist, und zwar um 35 Prozent auf 2,3 Millionen. Während dieser Zeit hat sich die Zahl derer fast verdoppelt, die gemäß der Volkszählung als „gemischte" oder „multiple" Ethnie beschrieben werden, von 660 000 im Jahr 2001 auf 1,2 Millionen 2011, was sie zur mit Abstand am schnellsten wachsende Kategorie macht.

Insgesamt ist beinahe einer von 10 Menschen in Großbritannien mit jemandem verheiratet, der nicht der eigenen ethnischen Gruppe angehört, oder lebt mit so jemandem zusammen, so die Analyse des Amtes für Nationale Statistik. [...]

Der Gegensatz zwischen Weißen und Menschen anderer Kulturen spiegelt sich in den Ergebnissen einer Studie der Social Integration Commission (Kommission für soziale Integration) wider, die Anfang der Woche veröffentlicht wurde. Diese Studie zeigte, dass weiße Menschen in ihrem Sozialleben am wenigsten mit Menschen anderer Ethnien zu tun haben.

Die Studie, die die Freundschaften von 4000 Personen untersuchte, stellte fest, dass eine typische weiße Person mit 50 Prozent weniger Menschen aus anderen ethnischen Gruppen verkehrt, als man erwarten könnte, wenn man die ethnische Struktur der Gegend berücksichtigt, in der sie lebt.

3.2
Revival of dead mines?

In Harlan County, Kentucky, there is a lot of coal. In Lynch, a village with around 10.000 people, there is nothing left. Maybe 200 people still live there. Obama's "Clean Power Plan" and cheaper gas have helped destroy the coal industry. Many of the locals believe that Trump will help the coal industry. In Lynch the average income is less than 20.000 dollars. So the revival of coal is what the people in Lynch are hoping for. Mining fossil fuels and protecting the environment is not a contradiction for them. Dee Davis, head of the office for environmental development, has a different opinion. He says that coal belongs to their past but not to their future. (116 words)

4 Produktion

Two topics are always in the news media: globalization and (the protection of) the environment. These two things are also the topic of the cartoon. In the cartoon there are five people. On the left-hand side there are three poor people who are probably form Africa and on the right-hand side there are two businessmen from the USA and the UK. They are both wearing shirts and ties and trousers. One of them, the American, has a cigar in his hand. Their body language tells us that the two Westerners think that they have the power over the others. They are making gestures of superiority. One of them, again the American, opens his hands in a generous gesture and is smiling. The three poor people have looks on their faces as if they cannot believe

what the two men are saying: "We all have to make sacrifices for the environment." Whereas the men use the common "we" it seems as if the only people who have to make sacrifices are the poor people in third-world-countries. Rich countries like the West exploit the natural resources of the poor countries. They become rich but don't share their wealth with the locals. We can see this in Nigeria, for example, a country rich in oil but where the majority of the population are poor. But this is not the only tragic thing. Some countries dump their toxic garbage in Africa, others ship their electronic garbage there. Thanks to the globalized world people in those poor countries can see very well what a luxurious life we are living and want to live a better life, as well. They have no perspectives in their own countries and come to our world, risking their lives on the way to get there. And what do we do? We let them drown or send them back. So I agree with the cartoonist saying that we live in a very cynical era. (323 words)

MUSTERPRÜFUNG 3

1 Hörverstehen

description of experiment	A man decided not to throw away trash for a whole year.
intended goal	He wanted to raise awareness about his carbon footprint.
success/development of the experiment	It is going well. After a year he has 50 kilos of garbage.
contents of the basement	plastic bottles, glass bottles, plastic and cardboards packaging.
contents of the paper box	bills and receipts
plans for the paper	he puts it in the shredder and then into the worm farm.
friends' suggestion what to do with some of the garbage	They suggested selling it on e-bay.
garbage as a symbol	It represents his footprint.

Transkript des Hörtextes

Reporter: We all produce garbage. It's inevitable! We consumer and throw away. Our food comes nicely wrapped in cellophane and plastic, or sealed in cans or glass. However, a young college student in California, Jim Donovan has decided to examine what garbage really is, or more in particular, to keep all his garbage for a whole year. Jim, why on earth are you keeping all your garbage?

Jim: Well, we all know that we throw away a ton of stuff, so I decided to keep it all in order to raise awareness about our carbon footprint, I've been trying to see what exactly it is that we chuck away.

Reporter: You've been doing it for a year now. How's it going?

Jim: It's going very well. I was really worried about how much space it would take up. Fortunately, we have a lot of space in the garage. But actually I have collected a lot less garbage than I thought. Right now I'm at 50 kilos of garbage, of stuff that would go straight to a landfill. The average American produces 700 kilos of garbage for the same amount of time. So I've produced significantly less. But even 50 kilos of garbage multiplied by 300 million Americans is an enormous amount.

Reporter: Where you surprised by how much less you produced than the average?

Jim: No, not really. Firstly, I am careful about what I buy, and secondly, when I started the experiment, I knew I had to be extra careful, otherwise the garage would have become a hellhole.

Reporter: So, let's see your garage, and see what you have after a year.

Jim: Here it is.

Reporter: OK ... Wow, it's not a lot of space. What does your mum say about it?

Jim: She's always supported me with my wild ideas. And she believes in protecting the environment. She just insisted that no food leftovers ended up here.

Reporter: OK, so what do you have here?

Jim: On this side we have plastic bottles and glass bottles. What you won't see are water bottles, because I pretty much refuse to drink bottled water. I don't drink sodas either, so it's not a lot.

Reporter: OK, what's this?

Jim: This is a container full of plastic and cardboard packaging.

Reporter: It's not that much.

Jim: There's not a lot of it, it's again just a matter of making choices about things, trying to use less ... Anyway, moving on, this is the paper box. There's no newspaper, it's all bills and receipts and so on ... I've pretty much reduced my junk mail to nothing, which I'm pretty happy about. I now get all my bills online so basically this pile isn't getting bigger anymore. A lot of this paper goes into the shredder there and then into the worm farm, because the worms eat the paper. They also eat all the food scraps from the kitchen. The worms turn it all into compost, which I'll use in the garden.

Reporter: What are you going to do with the rest of this stuff?

Jim: That's, that's a big question ... The year is nearly over and I'll take most of it to the recycling center myself. The garbage, which is actually in these two boxes right here, we haven't figured it out. My friends suggested selling it on eBay. Maybe that's not such a bad idea ...

Reporter: Really?

Jim: Yeah. I mean, if you look on eBay, there's weird stuff on eBay. Who knows what people might buy!

Reporter: Yeah, but isn't that just giving your garbage to someone else?

Jim: Well, you could see it as part of an environmental project and turn it into art.

Reporter: So what does this garbage represent to you?

Jim: Well, it represents my footprint. It's what I'm going to leave behind. Because this garbage, if I had thrown it away, it would have gone to the landfill, and it would basically be there for ever ... So I'm definitely proud when I look at these two small boxes and that's all of my garbage for a year ...

2 Leseverstehen

2.1

Omar's current occupation is *fighting for the Islamic State in Syria.*

The journalist Kermani talked to Omar *online.*

Omar told Kermani *shocking things about fighting in battles for the IS.*

Kermani's impression of Omar was that of a *polite and nice and friendly young man.*

Omar considers his childhood to have been *normal.*

Rashad Ali says that young men who tend to radicalism *think that the West did a lot of evil things and is to blame for everything.*

Omar thinks his task in Syria is to *liberate weak and oppressed women, children and elderly who have been neglected by the west.*

Ismael Lea South says the IS is "attractive" because *there is a feeling of brotherhood, just like in gangs – one takes care of the other.*

2.2

Young Muslims in Great Britain *feel that there is a gap between them and non-Muslims.*

3 Mediation

3.1

Verdienst junger Leute "angekratzt" (bedroht/einge-schränkt) durch ältere Arbeitnehmer, die länger im selben Job bleiben

Die Verdienstaussichten junger Menschen werden dauerhaft dadurch beschnitten, dass ältere Arbeitnehmer länger in ihren Jobs bleiben, sagt eine neue Studie. Jüngere Arbeitnehmer sind auch von einer generationsbedingten Veränderung betroffen, da ihre Arbeitsplätze unsicherer sind als die älterer Menschen, wie die Resolution Foundation Denkfabrik herausfand.

Die Anzahl junger Arbeitnehmer in „unsicherer" Arbeit ist drastisch gestiegen.

Die Unsicherheit hat zugenommen, da eine beträchtliche Minderheit sogenannte Null-Stunden-Arbeitsverträge hat, in unsicherer Selbstständigkeit ist, befristet oder Teilzeit beschäftigt ist, obwohl sie länger arbeiten wollen.

Paul Gregg, Professor für Wirtschaft und Soziales an der Universität Bath und Mitglied der Foundation sagte: „Die Menge an Zeit, die die Menschen im selben Job verbringen, nimmt stetig zu, besonders bei Frauen und älteren Arbeitnehmern. Aber es gibt auch Leute, die weniger häufiger den Job wechseln. Dies kann Beförderungen blockieren, was wiederum die Karriere junger Menschen behindert und ihre Einkünfte langfristig schmälern kann. Jobsicherheit ist entscheidend im Bestreben nach Vollbeschäftigung, da diese die Arbeit für diejenigen attraktiver macht, die die größten Hürden überwinden müssen. Aber wir sollten auch die sinkende Rate von Jobwechseln im Auge behalten, da diese ein wichtiger Weg für junge Arbeitnehmer sind, ihre Karrieren zu gestalten."

3.2
Minorities in Britain not well-integrated

Ethnic minorities are socially segregated and badly integrated, says a report. Politics is to blame for not having done enough for the growing numbers of immigrants. Ethnic minorities are often socially and economically isolated and hold cultural and religious values that are contrary to those of the British, so that often women don't have the basic rights British women should have. Often the authorities ignore the problem for fear of being accused of racism. In order to improve the situation it is recommended that immigrants swear an oath to uphold British values and that they take a language course. But it's not just the government that needs to work harder to integrate people – the immigrants themselves need to try harder. (120 words)

4 Produktion

Immigration is one of the main issues in all Western countries, as war, famine and the hope for a better life have forced people to move to richer countries. The acceptance of immigrants is the topic of the cartoon. In the cartoon there are three people talking, two men and one woman. One of the two men has dark skin and is obviously an immigrant. The man on the left is complaining that the immigrant should find a job instead of living on welfare. The immigrant says that he has actually just got a job, which he is starting the next day. The woman on the right then complains that he is taking away jobs from the locals. With these two statements you can see the prejudices immigrants are confronted with. Some people say immigrants just want to come to our countries and take money from the state and therefore they are seen as parasites. Other people are afraid that immigrants might take away their jobs. However, very often the jobs that immigrants are those that the locals refuse to do because they think they are too good for them. Immigrants rarely take away good jobs from locals. Furthermore, a lot of

locals live on welfare too, so it is unfair to criticize immigrants for that. In my opinion, immigrants face lots of problems in their new country due to the language barriers or their lack of skills. They have to adapt to a new culture and different values, so we should have more understanding for their situation. To conclude, it is unfair to criticize others if you do not know about the hardships they have lived through. (278 words)

MUSTERPRÜFUNG 4

1 Hörverstehen

British opinion of GM food	Their opinions are split. 34% think GM food is necessary, 27% consider it unsafe.
significance of this finding	First time the majority of the population supports GM food
types of GM products available in Britain	Soya beans, corn and cotton
purpose of those GM foods	The soya beans and the corn are fed to animals.
supporters' opinion of GM food	They say it improves crops because the plants are designed to resist damage from insects and chemicals.
people's thoughts on animal cloning	Most feel uncomfortable with it.
information about first cloned sheep	Called Dolly, born in 1996
legal status of food from cloned animals	the use of food or milk from cloned animals is forbidden by EU legislation
How this will change when Britain leaves the EU	It is uncertain whether the law will be changed.

Transkript des Hörtextes

In a recent opinion poll the British have shown that they have become more open to the idea of genetically engineered foods. Fifty-four percent of those surveyed said that they believed in principle that genetically modified food was necessary. Twenty-seven percent thought genetically modified foods were unsafe or unnecessary and should be completely banned.

This is the first time that the majority of the population supports the idea of GM food. But they weren't asked if they themselves would eat it. Just five years ago, the overwhelming majority of the population rejected the notion of any cloned food being used for any purpose at all in the country.

However, genetically-engineered soya beans, corn and cotton have been available in Britain for some time, despite not being produced here. Much of the corn and soya comes from the United States and is fed directly to animals which end up in the food chain. While one cannot buy GM corn in the shops, most of the meat sold in the supermarket aisles of the major chains will at some stage have been fed GM crops. Supporters say that the meat from these animals is totally safe. They say genetic engineering improves crops, as these crops are often designed to resist damage from insects or agricultural chemicals. Moreover, there is no evidence to support the fear that GM crops harm or affect animals in any way.

All food that may contain GM food, for example through feeding, must be labelled as GM food, so that consumers know what they are buying, but most people simply don't read labels.

Some companies market products as being free of genetically modified organisms in order to win over customers who are worried about GM food.

Another issue in recent times is animal cloning. The majority of the British public are still uncomfortable with the idea of animal cloning, and would refuse to eat or drink products that came from cloned animals. While most people know of Dolly, the first cloned sheep who was born in 1996, they are unaware of other animals that have been cloned. European legislation forbids the use of food or milk from cloned animals. At present, all cloned animals are just experimental projects.

Now that Britain has decided to leave the European Union, it is not known whether the law concerning GM food will be changed. Critics of GM food fear a lowering of consumer standards but as yet no one knows what will happen. Much will depend upon public opinion.

2 Leseverstehen

Was beschreibt der Begriff „Parallelleben"?	Die Trennung von asiatischen und weißen Gemeinden (in einigen Städten Nordenglands). Menschen unterschiedlicher Kulturen/Gruppen leben nicht in derselben Gegend, arbeiten nicht zusammen und nehmen auch nicht an denselben kulturellen oder sozialen Aktivitäten teil.
Welche Sorge hat der Autor?	dass sich seit 2001 nichts geändert hat
Welche Institution kann dieses Muster brechen?	die Schule
Wie soll diese Institution sein?	Ein sicherer Ort, an dem Schüler verschiedene Glaubensrichtungen/Familienverhältnisse kennenlernen, Erfahrungen teilen und Verbindungen herstellen
Welchem Fach wird mittlerweile weniger Priorität eingeräumt?	Staatsbürgerkunde // Das Fach, in dem Wissen über den Staat, die Demokratie und Zivilgesellschaft vermittelt wird.
Was sagen Psychologen über eine Gruppe Gleichgesinnter in einem Raum? Welche Schlussfolgerung kann man daraus für Schulen ziehen?	Gleiche Ansichten verstärken sich. Um dem (in der Schule) entgegenzuwirken, sollte man Lehrer und Schüler aus verschiedenen Kulturen/Gesellschaftsschichten zusammenbringen.
Wie ist die Situation in den Schulen laut Aussage des Autors?	Es gibt nach wie vor viele Schulen einer Kultur/Glaubensrichtung.
Wie fühlen sich Mitglieder muslimischer Gemeinden in Birmingham?	Sie fühlen sich ausgeschlossen und dämonisiert.

3 Mediation

3.1

Ist die typische amerikanische Familie ein Konzept der Vergangenheit?

In den 1950er Jahren hatte eine gewöhnliche Familie einen Ernährer, normalerweise den Vater, der morgens zur Arbeit ging und (spät) abends zurückkam. Die Mutter blieb zu Hause und kümmerte sich um die Familie. Ein Konzept, das man, wie wir alle wissen, heutzutage nicht mehr allzu oft sieht.

In einem Bericht, der vom Council on Contemporary Families veröffentlich wurde, heißt es, dass in den 1950er Jahren 65 Prozent aller Kinder unter 15 in einer solchen Familie lebten. Heute gilt dies nur für 22 Prozent. Viele Kinder leben heute in Familien, in denen beide Eltern arbeiten. Das nennt man einen Doppelverdienerhaushalt. Doch obwohl dies heutzutage das häufigste Konzept ist, trifft dies auch nur auf 34 Prozent aller Kinder zu. Wie also leben die anderen Kinder? Nun, beinahe ein Viertel aller Kinder, genauer gesagt 23 Prozent, wachsen bei einer alleinerziehenden Mutter auf. Aber gibt es auch alleinerziehende Väter? Ja, 3 Prozent leben bei einem alleinerziehenden Vater. 7 Prozent aller Kinder leben in einer Familie, in der der Vater oder die Mutter unverheiratet mit einem Partner zusammenlebt (der nicht der Vater/die Mutter des Kindes ist). Die restlichen 3 Prozent leben bei ihren Großeltern. Die Gründe für diese Umstände sind vielfältig. Die

Wirtschaft hat sich sehr verändert, die Menschen, und insbesondere Frauen, sind besser ausgebildet. Der Arbeitsmarkt für Frauen hat sich verbessert, was ihnen mehr Möglichkeiten eröffnet und mehr Unabhängigkeit gibt. Es gibt weniger Geschlechterdiskriminierung und die Sozialsysteme sind seit den 1960ern besser geworden.

Die wichtigste Tatsache jedoch ist, dass weniger Menschen heiraten. Während in den 1950ern zwei Drittel aller Haushalte Ehepaare mit Kindern waren, ist diese Zahl 2010 zurückgegangen auf 45 Prozent.

3.2
Rana Plaza hasn't changed a lot

When a textile factory collapsed three years ago killing 1000 people, international fashion promised improvements in the future and signed an action plan for better fire protection and more secure buildings. But since then more factories have burned down and more people have died – the last incident being an explosion at a packaging manufacturer. Human rights groups believe that foreign companies need to apply more pressure. However, the need to keep prices down and to uphold human rights do not always go together. Some international fashion companies now only want to produce in buildings that have been inspected by their own inspectors. (103 words)

4 Produktion

What to eat and what not to eat has become a complex philosophy nowadays. Some people go to organic shops, other people buy from the local farmers, but most people still buy in a supermarket. In Germany you can shop knowing that you won't buy GM food, but in countries like the USA you have to be very careful about what you are buying because it could very well be that the fruit or vegetables you selected are GM food. And do you really want to buy that?

There have been controversial debates about GM food or genetic engineering in general. Some people say that GM can solve problems like hunger and drought in poor countries, other people say that it can cause serious diseases like cancer. It is a fact that there are no long-term studies on the effect of the consumption on GM food which means that you have to think carefully about what you want to do and if you want to buy it.

A good thing about GM could be that you can add more vitamins or other things to food and make it even healthier. On the other hand, you might ask why we should interfere in nature and change things that are already perfect the way they are. Organic farmers fear that if GM farmers plant seeds, the pollen could fly over to their fields and "infect" the organic fields. GM farmers on the other hand might say that their crops don't need pesticides anymore because their crop is resistant towards pests.

Probably everybody has to make a decision for himself what to buy and what not to buy, but as long as people do not trust GM food, it is unlikely to be available in Germany. (293 words)

TRAINING

Teil A Hörverstehen

Transkript von Hörtext 1

Paul: Good afternoon, everyone, this is Paul Anthony and you are listening to Radio Orbit. It's time again for our daily program "Amanda, we need to talk". Nice to see you Amanda, by the way.

Amanda: Hi, everybody, and hello to you, dear Paul! What's our topic today?

Paul: Today I want to talk about … It is a topic that everybody talks about at the moment … It is about abolishing student fees.

Amanda: Incredible topic, Paul. Just imagine how incredible it would be if our students didn't have to take out student loans anymore and could just start their lives without being deeply in debt.

Grundlagen schaffen
1 das Abschaffen von Studiengebühren
2 zwei
3 C ein Gespräch
4 A freundlich

Transkript von Hörtext 2

Speaker 1: What is "globalization"? That's a very good question. Some economists say it's the integration of national economies into a single global economy. Transport allows us to ship goods across the world quickly and cheaply. This has led to a huge growth in cross-border trade and investment. This allows us all to buy what we want when we want it.

Speaker 2: To me, globalization has also got a lot to do with cultural integration. With the access to information around the world, firstly through satellite television and more recently through the internet, ideas can spread from one part of the world to another. Just look at the spread of American-style food, the English language and the western lifestyle.

Speaker 3: Globalization is bad for the little guy. In the USA we've seen the destruction of the clothing industry. The entire production of the world's clothes now takes place in Asia. The same is true of electronics and heavy industry. All our jobs are being outsourced to other parts of the world, and people are left behind living off benefits or in dead-end service jobs. We're getting a society divided between the well-off and the badly-paid. Many people feel they have no future.

Speaker 4: I think all this talk about globalization is aimed at creating a climate of fear and insecurity in high-wage economies like ours. The real aim is to get people to work longer hours for less money, in the hope that this will save their jobs. And it's also to blackmail the government into paying huge subsidies to firms willing to stay put, of course.

Speaker 5: The idea that globalization is the answer to world poverty is a complete sham. Look at China and India. A tiny minority benefits at the expense of the huge majority that is just as poor as it ever was. And what about Africa? They're worse off now than they were before! And when wages get too high in China or India, they'll move the jobs somewhere else.

Übung 1: Informationen entnehmen und auf Deutsch notieren

1/2 globalization: Globalisierung
integration: Integration
national economies: nationale Wirtschaften
single global economy: eine Weltwirtschaft
transport: Verkehrsmittel, Beförderungsmittel, Verbindungsmöglichkeiten, Transport
huge growth: enormes Wachstum
cross-border trade and investment: grenzüberschreitender Handel und grenzüberschreitende Investitionen

3	Was ist Globalisierung?	Das Verschmelzen nationaler Wirtschaften in eine Weltwirtschaft
	der Grund für Globalisierung	die schnellen Verkehrsmittel

4/5 cultural integration: kulturelle Integration
access to information: Zugang zu Informationen
satellite television: Satellitenfernsehen
the internet: das Internet
ideas can spread: Ideen können sich verbreiten
American-style food: amerikanisches Essen
the English language: die englische Sprache
the western lifestyle: der westliche Lebensstil

Globalisierung und Kultur	kulturelle Integration, z. B. Amerikanisierung bezogen auf Esskultur, Sprache und Lebensart

Übung 2: Informationen entnehmen und auf Englisch notieren

1 A outsourcing of jobs
2 destruction – clothing industry – production – jobs are being outsourced – living off benefits – dead-end service jobs – society divided – no future

3	people and jobs	Jobs are lost due to outsourcing. Americans are left with no jobs or dead-end jobs.

Übung 3: Die restliche Tabelle ausfüllen

Sprecher 4: Ziele des Sprechens über Globalisierung	ein Klima der Angst und Unsicherheit soll geschaffen werden; Menschen sollen für weniger Geld mehr arbeiten

Speaker 5: consequences of globalization	only few people benefit, others stay as poor as they were before; others are even worse than before

Transkript von Hörtext 3

Female presenter: Confusion and myths about climate change are widespread. There are many government leaders who insist that human-driven climate change is a hoax. Here are some of the most common misconceptions and the facts behind them. Number wOne:

Male presenter: The climate is always changing anyway. The world gets hotter and colder on a regular basis.

Female presenter: It's certainly true that the climate changes, but it does so at a very slow rate. The rate at which the climate is warming now is sudden and alarming. It is unparalleled in in human history, and could make the world such a hostile place that it won't be able to support life. So, number two:

Male presenter: Human activity can't really cause climate change.

Female presenter: Carbon dioxide is a major heat-trapping greenhouse gas. The concentration of carbon-dioxide in the atmosphere is now higher than at any point in the last 650,000 years. The majority of scientists are convinced that humans are affecting the climate by the way they live. Every study shows that today's temperatures could only be the result of human activity. Science has shown that greenhouse gases keep the earth warm, that there is evidence that concentrations of these gases are increasing, and that humans are responsible for these increases by burning fossil fuels and cutting down forests. Misconception number three:

Male presenter: It's too late to make a difference anyway.

Female presenter: The Intergovernmental Panel on Climate Change came to the conclusion that global emissions must decline to well below current levels by the middle of the century if we are to avoid dangerous climate change. It is possible to reduce global emissions with technologies that are available now. Putting off action to reduce greenhouse gases will make it more difficult and costly to reduce them in the future, as well as creating higher risks of severe climate change impacts. And finally, number four:

Male presenter: Climate change will make life more comfortable in the UK.

Female presenter: Climate change will lead to warmer winters, but temperatures will become uncomfortably hot in the summer, and the climate may also become less predictable. There's also the risk of rising sea levels and more frequent extreme weather like storms and floods. Tackling climate change now will make life a lot more comfortable.

Übung 1: Fragen auf Englisch beantworten

1 The concentration of carbon dioxide has increased in recent years.
2 We humans and our lifestyle are responsible for the changing climate because we burn fossil fuels and cut down forests.

Zu Frage 1: Die Frage lesen.
1   concentration, carbon dioxide
2   has changed; in recent years
3   present perfect

Zu Frage 1: Den Hörtext zuhören
1   now; any point in the last 650,000 year
2   is

Zu Frage 1: Die Antwort schreiben.
A, C und D können alle eingesetzt werden, aber A ist vom Stil her die beste Lösung.

Zu Frage 2: Die Frage lesen.
1   who (i.e. a person/people) responsible; changing climate
2   because

Zu Frage 2: Den Hörtext hören.
1   Menschen (humans are affecting the climate; today's temperatures could only be the result of human activity; humans are responsible)
2   Durch das Brennen von fossilen Brennstoff und das Abholzen von Wäldern

Zu Frage 2: Die Antwort schreiben
Humans are responsible for the changing climate because we burn fossil fuels and cut down forests.

Übung 2: Fragen auf Deutsch beantworten
1   Weil es sonst zu schwierig und zu teuer sein wird, und wir sonst unter schwierigen Wetterbedingungen zu leben haben.
2   Es wird wärmere Winter, aber auch heißere Sommer geben sowie ein weniger vorhersehbares und extremeres Wetter mit Stürmen und Überschwemmungen.

Frage 1
1   C   putting off action
2   1   It will make it more difficult to do anything in the future.
    2   It will be too costly to do anything.
    3   It will create higher risks of severe climate change impacts.

Frage 2
1   A   warmer winters: wärmere Winter
    C   uncomfortably hot in the summer: unangenehm heiß im Sommer
    E   less predictable: weniger vorhersehbar
    F   more frequent extreme weather like storms and floods: häufiger extremes Wetter wie Stürmen und Überschwemmungen

Transkript von Hörtext 4
Reporter: It's been six months since Julio's dad, Gerardo, was deported to Mexico. Recently, since the election of Donald Trump, there has been a clamp-down on people who moved to the USA illegally. While the government has always expelled illegal immigrants, it often turned a blind eye to people who had started businesses and families here in the USA. Julio's dad had lived here for 23 years before being deported, leaving behind his work, his wife and a teenage son, Julio, and a teenage daughter, Eva.

Eva: My family's life has never been the same since papa was deported. Our family is now divided, and our whole lives are about separation: we travel traffic back and forth, we're always saying hi and then goodbye, we're never just relaxing together – it's stressful. It's not the life any kid should live. Papa lives just two hours away so we try and visit often. Every time I see my dad, I get emotional. It's been a terrible time for us. When the agents came, I was asleep in bed ... the sound of police sirens outside woke me up. I was scared.

Presenter: It all started when Gerardo got a parking ticket. It became clear to the authorities that he had never registered himself in the USA as a legal resident. Within weeks he was deported to Mexico City – a 30-hour car drive from San Diego. Too far from his family to see them.

Julio: We're lucky. He now lives just on the other side of the border so he can be close to us in San Diego. He's got a job but it doesn't pay good. He worries about us a lot. It's also really hard for my mom.

Fernanda: I would talk to him about everyday things, like what needs to be fixed in the house, problems with the car. Now suddenly, I am the head of the household. I have to work twice as hard to make ends meet. Some nights I get home after 11 pm, so the boys have had to take on more responsibility in the household. It's like they lost both parents.

Julio: A lot of kids travel back and forth to Mexico. We're not the only divided family. My parents have talked about different options, like moving to Spain, so we can be together again, but with school and money, that's still up in the air. We live in hope, but until then we do what we can, using daily morning phone calls, text messages and weekend visits to hold us together. This is our normal routine.

Eva: The daily calls are nice, but I don't get hugs. We can't stop for breakfast together before school anymore. He always asks about school. He wants to know about my future and the letters from colleges. With college ahead and a career, I don't know if I will ever live with my father again.

Julio: Living without us has been bad for my dad. Yet as soon as we greet each other, it's like we were never apart. But still he is alone most of the time. I really miss not being a family anymore.

Presenter: And Julio's not the only one. Across America hundreds of kids have had a parent deported and their family split up.

Übung 1: *Multiple-Choice*-Aufgaben

1 B six months ago
"It's been six months since Julio's dad, Gerardo, was deported to Mexico."

2 A
1 He arrived in the USA illegally.
"It became clear to the authorities that he had never registered himself in the USA as a legal resident. Within weeks he was deported to Mexico City."
2 Gerardo got a parking ticket.
"It all started when Gerardo got a parking ticket."

3 A she becomes emotional
1 B
2 C
3 nicht im Text
4 A

4 C he wants to be near his family.
A "He's got a job but it doesn't pay good."
B "Mexico City is a 30-hour car drive from San Diego."

Übung 2: Eine Fortsetzung schreiben

1 The mother's new role is head of the household.
1 "Now suddenly, I am the head of the household." ("head of household" ist die neue Rolle)
2 "I have to work twice as hard to make ends meet."
3 "Some nights I get home after 11 pm."

2 One possibility for the future is that they all move to Spain.
1 A option
2 Julio sagt folgendes: Meine Eltern haben über die Möglichkeit gesprochen, nach Spanien umzuziehen.
3 Two things Eva misses are hugs and breakfast together before school.
1 A daily calls
C hugs
D breakfast before school
F her future
H college
I career
2 "I don't get hugs. We can't stop for breakfast together before school anymore." Also: "hugs" und "breakfast before school".

Übung 3: Aussagen zuordnen

1 Folgende Person redet nicht: Gerardo.
2
1 separation
2 dad/father/papa; worry
3 hard; mum
4 talk/speak; everyday things
5 children/kids; lose/lost; both parents
6 live; dad; never/ever
7 hundreds of kids/children; parent deported

1	Our whole lives are about separation.	c	Eva
2	Our dad worries about us a lot.	d	Julio
3	Life has become hard for our dad.	d	Nicht im Text, auch wenn das Leben doch schwierig für den Vater ist. Julio sagt, dass das Leben für seine Mutter härter geworden ist.
4	I still talk to Gerardo about everyday things.		Not in text: Fernanda used to talk to Gerardo about everyday things
5	I feel that the children have lost both their parents.	e	Fernanda
6	I feel I may never live with my dad again	c	Eva
7	There are hundreds of kids in the USA who have had one parent deported.	b	presenter

Teil B Leseverstehen

1 Multiple Choice

Übung 1: Genau lesen

1 B Because they are worried about the effects on a legendary forest and in particular a famous old tree.
A Ll. 15–20. Hier wird indirekt Sherwood Forest erwähnt.
B Sie sind für „fracking" (ll. 6–11): Ineos and the Foresty Commission have agreed terms to start searching for shale gas.
C 200 Meter (ll. 17–18)
D Major Oak: ist „in folklore" mit „Robin Hood and his merry men" verbunden. Ineos wird wahrscheinlich 200m entfernt arbeiten.
E Es wird erwähnt, dass die Proben nicht weit entfernt von der Eiche, die mit Robin Hood assoziiert wird, stattfinden werden.
Tourismus wird nicht erwähnt. Später im Text folgt die Aussage zur ikonischen Bedeutung des Sherwood Forest, jedoch nicht zu Sherwood Forest als Touristenmagnet.
F Ll. 15–20: Die *Fracking-Arbeiten* sollen nicht weit entfernet vom Baum stattfinden, und könnten Auswirkungen auf den Wald, und damit auch auf den Baum haben.

Übung 2: Genau lesen

2 C It has caused a lot of angry public discussion and disagreement, but only a view are protesting against it.

A Ll. 20–42; hier geht es um fracking und die Reaktionen dazu.

B Die erste Teilaussage ("It is widely accepted as being good for the country") steht nicht im Text.

C excited = aufgeregt
nein

D controversial: umstritten
Bislang nur: "A small protest camp has been established" (l. 30)

E Nein: Es gab einige Tests (l. 25), aber es wird von „mistakes" (l. 40) gesprochen.
Nein: Es ist immer noch „controversial" (l, 25).

F Fracking ist immer noch umstritten, aber nur eine kleine Gruppe protestiert sichtbar dagegen.

Übung 3: Selbstständig arbeiten.

Die Aussage steht in ll. 49–53:
The firm's shale operations director, Tom Pickering, said: "Potentially we in the UK have a huge supply of indigenous gas under our own feet. It would be simply crazy not to explore this natural resource."

A Es wird nicht erwähnt, ob die Ressourcen knapp sind oder nicht.

B „A huge supply" wird erwähnt, allerdings in Verbindung mit „potentially", d.h. wir kennen das wahre Ausmaß nicht.

C Dies ist die richtige Lösung: Wir kennen das Ausmaß der Vorkommen nicht („potentially"). Die Tests sollen genau das herausfinden.

D Man kann vermuten, dass es teuer und kompliziert ist, Gas zu finden, aber dies wird nicht im Text erwähnt.

2 Ausfüllen einer Tabelle

Übung 1: Ausfüllen einer Tabelle mit Informationen auf Englisch

A

Changes President Trump initiated:
Consequences of those changes:

B

"This is what this is all about," Trump said today at the Environmental Protection Agency headquarters. "Bringing back our jobs, bringing back our dreams and making America wealthy again."

[...] As part of the roll-back, Trump will initiate a review of the Clean Power Plan, which restricts greenhouse gas emissions at coal-fired power plants. The regulation [...] has been the subject of long-running legal challenges by Republican-led states and those who profit from burning oil, coal and gas.

Trump, who has called global warming a 'hoax' invented by the Chinese, has repeatedly criticized the power-plant rule and others as an attack on American workers and the struggling US coal industry.

[...] Trump repeated that point saying, "We're going to have safety, we're going to have clean water, we're going to have clean air, but so many [regulations] are unnecessary and so many are job-killing."

[...] In addition to pulling back from the Clean Power Plan, the administration will also lift a 14-month-old moratorium on new coal leases on federal lands. [...] Trump accused his predecessor of waging a "War on Coal" and boasted in a speech to Congress that he has made "a historic effort to massively reduce job-crushing regulations," including some that threaten "the future and livelihoods of our great coal miners". [...]

C	Information from the text
Changes President Trump initiated:	– clean Power Plan will be reviewed – moratorium on new coal leases on federal lands will be lifted – removal of regulations
Consequences of those changes:	– Trump will bring back jobs and revive the American Dream – Revival of coal industry – safety, clean water and jobs

Übung 2: Ausfüllen einer Tabelle mit Informationen auf Deutsch

A

Wie kommentiert Trump die Erderwärmung und Umweltschutzgesetze?
Wie sieht der Opposition die Folgen der Veränderungen?

B

Trump, who has called global warming a 'hoax' invented by the Chinese, has repeatedly criticized the power-plant rule and others as an attack on American workers and the struggling US coal industry. [...]

The Obama administration, some Democratic-led states and environmental groups countered that it will spur thousands of clean-energy jobs and help the US meet ambitious goals to reduce carbon pollution set by the international agreement signed in Paris. [...] According to an Energy Department analysis released in January, coal mining now accounts for fewer than 70,000 US jobs. [...] Former Vice President Al Gore, who met with Trump at Trump Tower during the transition, called the president's move today a "misguided step away from a sustainable, carbon-free future for ourselves and generations to come."

C

Englisch	Deutsch
hoax	Falschmeldung
struggling	angeschlagen
spur	befeuern
account for	betragen
misguided	fehlgeleitet
sustainable	nachhaltig

D

	Information from the text
Wie kommentiert Trump den Erderwärmung?	– Trump sagt, dass die Chinesen die Erderwärmung erfunden haben – Es ist eine Attacke auf amerikanischen Arbeiter und die Kohlenindustrie.
Wie sieht die Opposition die Folgen der Veränderungen?	– Der Weg führt weg von einer nachhaltigen, CO2 freien Zukunft

3 Sätze vervollständigen

1 Beim ersten: „neglecting basics". Basics = everyday essential things
Lösung: One of the symptoms of internet addiction is not doing everyday essential things like eating and sleeping.

2 A highly educated, introverted men
B middle-aged women on home computers
Gruppe A ist bereits in früheren Studien als internetsüchtig aufgefallen.
Lösung: It used to be thought that internet addicts were mostly highly educated, introverted men but new research shows that actually it is middle-aged women on home computers who are more likely to be addicted to the internet.

3 thrombosis = blood clots (ll. 30–31)
Lösung: There have been cases of people dying from thrombosis because they stayed seated for too long in internet cafes. (Achten Sie darauf, dass ein Verb – „stayed" – statt dem Gerundium – „staying" – verwendet werden muss.)

4 alarm
Lösung: In South Korea there are worries about the large number of pupils who drop out of school and people who quit their jobs to spend more time on their computers.

Teil C Mediation und Übersetzung (Translation)

1 Aufgabentyp Übersetzung: Einen Text ins Deutsch übersetzen

Übung 1: Den Text verstehen

English	German
long-standing	langjährig
host society	gastgebende Gesellschaft; Aufnahmeland
to adapt	sich anpassen
though	jedoch
the latter	Letzterer/Letztere/Letzteres
strike a balance	ein Gleichgewicht einhalten
to cluster together	zusammenhängen, sich zusammengruppieren
to require	erfordern
appealing	reizvoll
obstacles	Hindernisse
trust	Vertrauen

Übung 2: Satz für Satz übersetzen

1 Wenn es darum geht, Einwanderer zu integrieren, *ist Freundschaft der Schlüssel.*

2 *Wie integriert man* Neuankömmlinge und sogar langjährige Einwohner, *die immer noch für sich leben, in die britische Gesellschaft?*

3 *Zunächst handelt es sich um einen zweiseitigen Prozess:* sowohl die Aufnahmegesellschaft als auch der Zugezogene müssen sich anpassen, wenngleich *sich* letzterer *mehr anstrengen muss.*

4 *Zweitens muss ein Gleichgewicht* eingehalten werden, *und zwar zwischen der Tatsache, dass sich Menschen ähnlicher Herkunft gern* zusammenhängen, *und dem Glauben, dass sich eine gute Gesellschaft* über soziale und ethnische Grenzen hinweg *durchmischen und miteinander teilen* muss.

5 Wenige Briten *sagen, dass sie keinen Nachbarn* einer unterschiedlichen/anderen Rasse *haben wollen, und* lediglich ungefähr 30 Prozent der Leute *sagen, sie würden lieber in einer Gegend leben,* in der alle die gleiche Herkunft haben.

6 Eine reizvolle Definition *einer integrierten Gesellschaft ist die, in der* beinahe jeder ein möglicher Freund ist: *Unterschiede in Bezug auf Rasse, Klasse und Religion sind* keine Hindernisse *für persönliches* Vertrauen, *Loyalität und sogar Intimität zwischen Individuen* unterschiedlicher Herkunft.

Übung 3: Eine Übersetzung beurteilen und überarbeiten

A

Wenn **es dazu kommt (Ausdruck),** Einwanderer zu integrieren, ist Freundschaft der Schlüssel

Wie integriert man **Neukommer (Ausdruck)** und sogar **lange stehende (Ausdruck)** Bewohner, die immer noch für sich leben, in die britische Gesellschaft?

Zunächst **ist (Ausdruck)** es sich ein zweiseitiger Prozess: beide, die Gastgeber-Gesellschaft und die Hinzukommenden müssen sich anpassen, doch der zuletzt **kommende (Ausdruck)** muss das umso mehr tun.

Zweitens gibt es ein Gleichgewicht, dass es einzuhalten **gibt (Ausdruck)** zwischen **der Akzeptanz (Ausdruck),** dass Leute mit ähnlichem Hintergrund **zusammenkleben (Ausdruck)** wollen und dem Glauben, dass eine gute Gesellschaft mehr **erforderte (Grammatik)** als ein bisschen **Mixen und Teilen (Ausdruck)** über soziale und ethnische Linien hinweg.

Wenige **Britische (Rechtschreibung) Menschen (Ausdruck)** sagen, dass sie niemanden von einer anderen Rasse als Nachbarn haben wollen und nur ungefähr 30 Prozent dieser Menschen sagen, sie **werden (Grammatik)** lieber in einer Gegend leben, wo **jeder ist vom selben Hintergrund (Satzbau).**

Eine ansprechende Definition einer integrierten Gesellschaft ist eine, in der **meistens (Ausdruck)** jeder ein **potenter (Ausdruck)** Freund ist: Unterschiede zwischen Rasse, Klasse und Religion sind keine Hindernisse für persönliches Vertrauen, Loyalität und sogar Intimität zwischen Individuen verschiedenen Hintergrunds.

B Mögliche Lösung:

Wenn es darum geht, Einwanderer zu integrieren, ist Freundschaft der Schlüssel

Wie integriert man Neuankömmlinge und sogar langjährige Einwohner, die immer noch für sich leben, in die britische Gesellschaft?

Zunächst handelt es sich um einen zweiseitigen Prozess: sowohl die gastgebende Gesellschaft als auch der Neuankömmling müssen sich anpassen, jedoch ist es so, dass sich letzterer mehr anstrengen muss. Zweitens gibt es ein Gleichgewicht, das es einzuhalten gilt zwischen der Tatsache, dass man akzeptieren muss, dass Leute mit ähnlicher Herkunft gern zusammenbleiben werden und dem Glauben, dass sich eine gute Gesellschaft über soziale und ethnische Grenzen hinweg durchmischen und miteinander teilen muss. Wenige Briten sagen, dass sie niemanden einer anderen Rasse als Nachbarn haben wollen und lediglich ungefähr 30 Prozent der Leute sagen, sie würden lieber in einer Gegend leben, in der jeder dieselbe Herkunft hat. Eine reizvolle Definition einer integrierten Gesellschaft ist eine, in der beinahe jeder ein möglicher Freund ist: Unterschiede zwischen Rasse, Klasse und Religion sind keine Hindernisse für persönliches Vertrauen, Loyalität und sogar Intimität zwischen Individuen verschiedener Herkunft.

2 Aufgabentyp Mediation: Einen Text auf Englisch zusammenfassen

Übung 1: Den Text lesen und verstehen.

Zeilen-nummern	Zusammenfassung auf Deutsch
1–5	*So viel landet im Müll; die Beteiligten; die Auswirkungen*
6–22	Geringschätzung von Lebensmitteln; Geiz-ist-geil-Mentalität
23–28	Trend zu Fast Food und Fertigprodukten aus Zeitgründen
29–40	Abfälle vermeiden; bewusster Umgang; positive Konsequenzen

Übung 2: Unwichtiges herausstreichen

Lebensmittel: Zwischen Wertschätzung und Verschwendung

Jahr für Jahr landen in Deutschland 11 Millionen Tonnen Lebensmittel im Wert von circa 25 Milliarden Euro im Müll. [...]

Zur Verschwendung tragen alle bei: Hersteller, Landwirtschaft, Handel und Verbraucher.

Der verschwenderische Umgang mit Lebensmitteln wirkt sich negativ sowohl auf die Umwelt und die Ressourcen als auch die Versorgung vor allem der Bevölkerung in den ärmeren Ländern aus.

Aus der Wertschätzung von Lebensmitteln ist inzwischen eher eine Geringschätzung geworden. Zurückzuführen ist dies auf den ständigen Preiskampf des Lebensmitteleinzelhandels in Deutschland. In der Folge sind die Ausgaben für Nahrungs- und Genussmittel von 1950 mit 50 Prozent des Haushaltseinkommens auf aktuell nur noch 9,5 Prozent gesunken. Lebensmittel sind immer billiger geworden. Und die „Geiz ist Geil"-Mentalität wird weiter geschürt, denn es vergeht kein Tag ohne Werbung mit neuen Sonderangeboten.

Der Trend zu Fast Food und Fertigprodukten hält ungebrochen an. Der veränderte Alltag und die Zeitknappheit haben dazu geführt, dass inzwischen fast 40 Prozent der Lebensmittelausgaben in der Außer-Haus-Verpflegung erfolgen – mit steigender Tendenz. [...]

Wer beim Einkauf und auch zu Hause einige Tipps beherzigt, kann dazu beitragen, dass weniger Nahrungsmittel verschwendet werden. [...]

~~Wir alle können jedoch schon heute damit beginnen, denn über die Hälfte aller Lebensmittelabfälle im Haushalt ist vermeidbar.~~ Ein bewusster Umgang mit Lebensmitteln kann zu Einsparungen von 230 Euro pro Person und mehr führen. ~~Damit tun Sie nicht nur Gutes für den Umwelt- und Klimaschutz, sondern schonen gleichzeitig Ihren Geldbeutel.~~

Übung 3: Beantworten von Wh-Fragen auf Englisch

1. 11 million tons of food go to waste every year.
2. Manufacturers, farmers, retail and consumers are responsible for this waste.
3. This waste has negative consequences for the environment and resources and also for the food supply in poorer parts of the world.
4. If you are more responsible with food, you can save 230€ per person and more.
5. a People don't value food anymore.
   b They spend less and less money on it.
6. People eat fast food and convenience/ready-made food, as people don't have much time anymore.

Übung 4: Einen fertigen Text schreiben

11 million tons of food go to waste every year. Manufacturers, farmers, retail and consumers are responsible for this waste. The waste has negative consequences for the environment and resources and also for the supply of food in poorer parts of the world. If you are more responsible with food, you can save € 230 per person and more. Unfortunately, people don't value good food anymore. You can see that they spend less and less money on it – currently only 9.5 per cent of the household income. Because people don't have time anymore, many of them buy fast food and convenience food. 40 per cent of expenses for food are for eating out. (112 words)

Produktion

Das Verfassen eines Kommentars zu einem Thema

Übung 1: Die Aufgabenstellung verstehen

A a possible radicalization of young Muslims; ways to prevent
B name, describe
C name: nennen
describe: beschreiben

Übung 2: Ideen sammeln

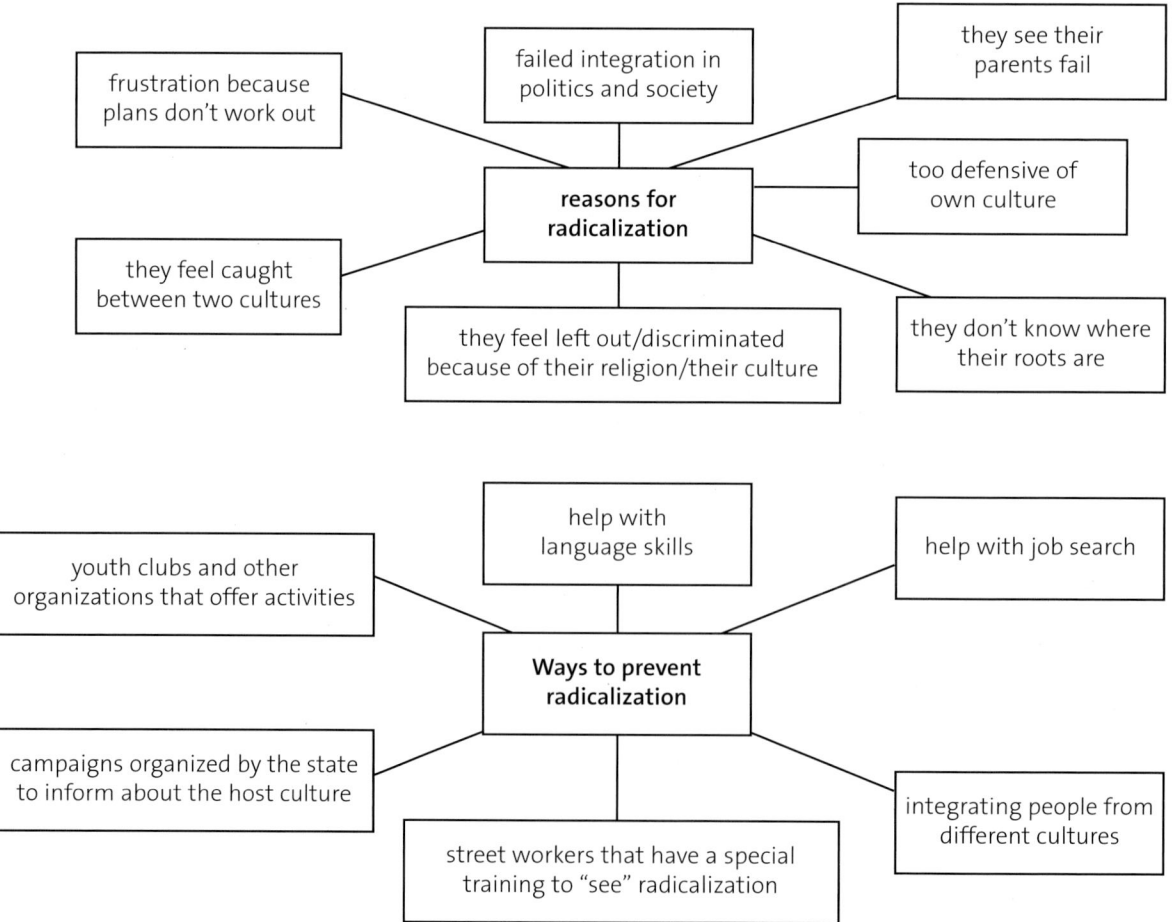

Übung 3: Eine Gliederung erstellen

the reasons for a possible radicalization of young Muslims	
reason	**examples**
frustration because plans don't work out	their school grades are not good enough; language skills not good enough
They feel left out/discriminated against because of their religion/their culture.	other people/groups are biased and exclude Muslims; they don't know how to make their culture/religion part of the country they live in
Caught between cultures, they feel they must defend their parents' culture.	They become too defensive of anything in their culture and support extreme versions of it.

ways to prevent radicalization	
idea	**examples**
programs at school to help with problems	help with homework, job application training
youth clubs and other organisations that offer activities integrating people from different cultures	
People who have a special training to "see" when radicalization starts	social workers
campaigns organized by the state to inform about (the) other culture(s)	programmes on TV, cultural programmes

Übung 4: Den Text schreiben

A

Das Thema einleiten	Die eigene Meinung darlegen	Punkte/Argumente auflisten
It makes sense to start by asking whether ... The issue I want to discuss here is ...	In my opinion, ... I am of the opinion that ...	Firstly, ... Secondly, ... Finally, ... First of all ...

Eine These untermauern	Ausnahmen einräumen	Ein Gegenargument anführen
In addition , ... Moreover, ... Furthermore, ... Another point to consider is this:	except for ... apart from ... although ... even though ...	On the other hand, ... However, ... In spite of this, ...
Einen Standpunkt begründen	**Auswirkungen oder Resultate beschreiben**	**Die Argumentation zusammenfassen und ein Fazit ziehen**
That is why ... For this reason ...	Therefore, ... As a result, ... As a consequence, ... Because of this, ...	To sum up, ... On the whole, ... In conclusion, ... We can clearly see that ...

B

There are many reasons why radicalization takes place. First of all, some youngsters feel frustrated when their plans for the future don't work out. They might not get job or training offers because they don't have good grades or speak the local language well, so they see no future for themselves. Secondly, they feel discriminated against because of their religion or culture. On the one hand, many employers don't want to employ people who are different. On the other hand, many Muslims live separately from the host nation. Finally, youngsters often feel that they have to defend their own culture, which is seen as being different. As a consequence, youngsters become radicalized by an extreme understanding of their religion.

How to prevent radicalization is a difficult subject. First of all, schools could offer extra classes for those who have problems with the language (or with other subjects) or courses on how to apply for jobs. Secondly, youth and sport clubs should get more involved with schools. These clubs could bring cultures together and encourage cross-cultural understanding. Thirdly, there should be people who are trained in working with people of different cultures and who can "see" when radicalization starts. Social workers, for example, have special training and can see radicalization when it begins. Finally, the state could start programmes about different cultures to pave the way for communication and to fight bias, prejudice and lack of information. New TV programmes and more state-sponsored cultural programmes could help.
(246 Wörter)

Übung 5: Eine Einleitung und einen Schluss formulieren

A   Beurteilung: Es fehlen zwar Informationen zur Terror-attacke, und dennoch ist es ein guter Einstieg. Der zweite Satz ist zu persönlich; Er sollte neutraler formuliert sein.

Bessere Version: In 2017 a young radicalized Muslim killed many people in a suicide bomb attack in Manchester. It is often asked why youngsters are being radicalized and what can we do to prevent this. In this essay I want to explore these two issues.

B   Beurteilung: Zu lang. Man darf nur „in conclusion" oder „to sum up" verwenden, aber nicht beides. Die Gründe für die Radikalisierung sowie die Auflistung der Präventionsmethoden werden nochmals aufgeführt – Details gehören jedoch nicht in den Schlussteil. Der erste und der letzte Satz sind ausreichend und treffend formuliert.

Bessere Version: In conclusion, I would like to say that not enough has been done to integrate young Muslims. It should be our aim that youngsters feel both proud to be Muslim and proud to be part of our society.

2 Das Schreiben einer Diskussion

Übung 1: Die Aufgabenstellung verstehen

A   economic, the West benefits, globalization
B   discuss (pros and cons)
C   discuss: erörtern

Übung 2: Argumente sammeln und ordnen

"In economic terms, only the West benefits from globalisation."	
a globalised world is good	a globalised world is bad
My opinion: a globalised world is good	My opinion: a globalised world is bad (x)
1 outsourcing creates jobs 2 we can all benefit from cooperation 3 due to competition consumers have better options (prices etc.)	1 local workers are not paid well and are exploited 2 consumers in developing countries don't benefit and have no access to the produced goods 3 the West exports products and therefore destroys the market in developing countries

Übung 3: Beispiele finden

Argument 1: Outsourcing creates jobs.
Example: When a company decides to produce abroad, those workers are normally from the country the company moves production to.

Argument 2: We can all benefit from cooperation.
Example: Exchange of knowledge is possible.
Argument 3: Due to competition consumers have better options (prices, etc.).
Example: prices, wider product range
Gegenargument 1: Local workers are not paid well and are exploited.
Example: sweat shops in Bangladesh
Gegenargument 2: Consumers in developing countries don't benefit and have no access to the produced goods.
Example: Products are still too expensive for them and don't reach the local markets/are not made for local markets.
Gegenargument 3: The West exports products and therefore destroys the market in developing countries.
Example: Exporting chicken pieces to Africa Europeans don't want to eat; European chickens are cheaper than the local chickens.

Übung 4: Eine fertige Diskussion sortieren

A

1	I would like to start with the fact that we all benefit from cheaper prices – and not just the people in the West. Because there is a global market there is a wider selection of products we can choose from. This competition is good for the customer who can look for the best price of a product.
2	Additionally, I would like to mention that outsourcing can be a job generator in many countries. If a company didn't go to another country for production, for example, there wouldn't be any new jobs.
3	On the other hand we have to admit that many companies exploit the workers in developing countries. They pay them very low wages and therefore they can keep production costs low and this has an effect on the price of a product.
4	Moreover, many people in the West don't have a job anymore because a company moved to another country.

B   Arguments 1–3 are good. Some examples would be good. Argument 4 could be more detailed and again an example would be good.

C   I would like to start with the fact that we all benefit from cheaper prices – and not just the people in the West. Because there is a global market there is a wider selection of products we can choose from. This competition is good for the customer who can look for the best price of a product. If several companies, for example, produce a fan, I can choose the cheapest one and order it from wherever it is produced.
Additionally, I would like to mention that outsourcing can be a job generator in many countries. If a company

didn't go to another country for production, for example, there wouldn't be any new jobs. A couple of years ago Nokia moved their production department to Romania. They got subsidies from that country and also hired a lot of locals.

On the other hand, many companies exploit workers in third-world-countries. They pay them very low wages so that they can keep production costs low and the price of a product cheaper. A good example are the sweat shops in Asian countries. Women, and often children, work there in poor conditions for very little money. The result is that Westerners can buy very cheap clothes – but for the locals these products are still not affordable. Furthermore, many people in the West don't have job anymore as many companies have moved to another country. What is an advantage for one person can be a disadvantage for another person. When Nokia moved their production to Romania, many people in the West lost their jobs.

Übung 5: Eine gute Einleitung schreiben
A Further ideas: fire in a sweat shop in Bangladesh; protest of workers; suicides in Chinese factories
B *The number of Africans crossing the Mediterranean is increasing dramatically. If Africans are prepared to leave their countries and face death to move to the West, is it true that only the West is benefiting economically from globalization?*
(Beachten Sie, dass die Einleitung immer bei ca. 40 Wörtern liegen sollte.)

Übung 6: Einen passenden Schluss schreiben
A Der Schluss ist an sich gut; lediglich der letzte Satz sollte optimiert werden, damit der Appell nicht zu salopp klingt. Die Länge stimmt.
B *To conclude, I would like to stress the fact that many companies exploit workers in developing countries. It is up to us as consumers to make our feelings known by not buying cheap products.*
(Beachten Sie, dass der Schluss immer bei ca. 40 Wörtern liegen muss.)

3 Beschreibung und Interpretation eines Bildes/Cartoons/Diagrams

Übung 1: Die Aufgabenstellung verstehen
A overconsumption, consequences for humanity
B describe, interpret
C describe: beschreiben
Interpret: interpretieren

Übung 2: Beschreibung des Cartoons: Notizen machen
Car driving up a hill; driving on the road to the future, car is an SUV, three people (family) sitting in it, car uses a lot of gas (see exhaust), the road becomes bumpy, woman is worried, man isn't, woman says the lifestyle of the consumers destroys the road, man tells her not to worry

because they really have a good car and so they won't notice the condition of the road

Übung 3: Welche Informationen stimmen?
3 The road turns from smooth to rough.
4 The man is driving an SUV.
5 The car is driving on a symbolic road.
6 The car stands for something else.
8 The man who is driving the car is trying to calm his wife down.
9 The man is happy about his car because with it they don't notice the bumpy road.

Übung 4: Die zentrale Aussage des Cartoons bestimmen
A/B

1	People consume too much.	true for many people but not for everybody
2	People have a bad conscience about destroying the environment.	again not true for everybody
3	We are destroying our earth but instead of stopping the madness we invent more and more things for our convenience.	but we also invent things that help the planet
4	Overconsumption destroys the earth.	This reflects the comment of the woman but not of the man.
5	People try to ignore the damage they do to the environment.	The man implies that by buying a better product, he can manage to ignore the destruction he is creating.
6	The roads are in a devastating state and something has to be done about it.	not the topic of the cartoon at all

Übung 5: Die Beschreibung und die Interpretation verfassen
Introduction:
This is a cartoon about the environment.
Description:
In the cartoon there is an SUV with a family sitting in it that is driving up a road that was smooth and is becoming bumpy. There is a sign by the road that says "Road to the future". In the very back a child is sitting looking out of the window. The wife/mother is sitting in the back seat while the husband/father is driving. The parents are talking to each other. The woman says that the "weight of our

consumer lifestyles" is responsible for the bad road conditions. The husband doesn't have a bad conscience. He tells his wife not to worry about the road because they have such a good car.

Analysis:

The cartoonist is criticizing people who don't worry about their consumer lifestyle and the consequences for the environment. Instead, they adapt to the changing conditions by consuming even more.

Your opinion:

The cartoonist certainly has a point. Instead of consuming less and protecting the environment we consume more. Instead of doing something against global warming we buy better fans to withstand the heat. What we should do is try to live with less. We all have things that we don't really need. We only think we need them – for status reasons or for convenience. If we all had less cars (in the family), used less electricity, lived more responsibly, we could easily make this world a better place.